THE
NEW APOSTOLIC
AGE

MICHAEL SHENTON

The New Apostolic Age by Michael Shenton

This book is written to provide information and motivation to readers. Its purpose is not to render any type of psychological, legal, or professional advice of any kind. The content is the sole opinion and expression of the author, and not necessarily that of the publisher.

Copyright © 2022 by Michael Shenton

All rights reserved. No part of this book may be reproduced, transmitted, or distributed in any form by any means, including, but not limited to, recording, photocopying, or taking screenshots of parts of the book, without prior written permission from the author or the publisher. Brief quotations for noncommercial purposes, such as book reviews, permitted by Fair Use of the U.S. Copyright Law, are allowed without written permissions, as long as such quotations do not cause damage to the book's commercial value.

ISBN: 978-1-951670-51-1 (Paperback)
ISBN: 978-1-951670-52-8 (Digital)

Printed in the United States of America.

DEDICATION

I dedicate this book to my Wife Diane, my Daughter Jenna, and my Son Alec.

I thank them for all the Love and Support I have received from them while on my Spiritual Journey.

I thank my mum for her support through the years. I also thank all the Christians in the Churches in the area who supported my family and me. I thank the Holy Spirit and Jesus who wrote this book.

CONTENTS

INTRODUCTION VII
CHAPTER 1 The Vision 1
CHAPTER 2 Spending Time with God 5
CHAPTER 3 Being Filled with the Holy Spirit 15
CHAPTER 4 Being Filled with the Spirit of Elijah 25
CHAPTER 5 Being Baptized with Fire 33
CHAPTER 6 The Keys to the Apostolic Anointing 41
CHAPTER 7 The Gifts of the Holy Spirit 71
CHAPTER 8 The Works 97
CHAPTER 9 The Persecution 137
CHAPTER 10 The Desert Experience-Being Tested 153
CHAPTER 11 The Blessing 163
CHAPTER 12 Being Full of the Holy Spirit 171
CHAPTER 13 Revival 175

CHAPTER 14 God's Plan for His Church...........181
CHAPTER 15 Home Group Meetings...........195
CHAPTER 16 The Mistakes...........199
CHAPTER 17 Scripture References and Notes...........211
ABOUT THE AUTHOR...........229

INTRODUCTION

My motive in writing this book is to encourage you on your spiritual journey.

Does spiritual growth cost anything—of course, it does, but it is not complicated? I have written this book to understand that I am not special or more holy than anyone else.

All the personal experiences I will unfold in this book have come about for one very simple reason, I have spent time in God's presence. I have not earned the experiences by doing some mighty act for God, nor have I earned them by being someone special. I repeat that all the beautiful experiences have happened to me because I spent time with God; they were a gift of his love and grace to a friend.

Please do not think that when I share an experience in this book, I am boasting, I want you to understand that you can experience the same and even greater things no matter who you are. I pray and know that you will have the same experiences and even greater experiences and perform even greater works with God's assistance. I am willing to state that my walk with God has not been perfect and has been riddled with disobedience and rebellion, as have all God's Children. I only know one person with no son, whose name is Jesus.

When I share some of the things of God in this book, please understand that I have no power or goodness of my own, and without the Holy Spirit, I could do nothing.

If I will not bore you, I would like to explain a little bit of my past so you will understand some of the things I will say further in this book.

I was brought up in Swansea, the U.K., in a council house estate, I was very advanced for my age, and at the age of 4, I decided I wanted to go to Sunday school. I went to Sunday School until the age of 7. At age 7, I joined the church choir and went to Church 3 times a day: morning, evening, and Sunday school.

Going to Church 3 times a day continued until I was nearly 12. I then became a Server and served in morning or evening services until 15. The church I was in was the Church of Wales, equivalent to an Anglican or Church of England background.

What I am going to say now may disturb some people. In all this time of going to church, I never knew Jesus, I never encountered God either in the services or in my life, nor did God speak to me. None of my friends or older people in the church ever talked of an encounter with God or any spiritual experience.

I never saw God act or anyone healed in or outside of the church in all this time. I never heard of being filled with the Holy Spirit, nor did my friends or acquaintances.

After fifteen, a lady named Joan Winter, who was my Music Teacher and had been my Church

Choir Mistress for many years, died suddenly. I am not sure of her age, but I would guess 23, and she had only been married a short time.

The Church Priest came to see me and tell me the news. I remember being very angry and upset, I said I did not believe in a God that could allow such a thing to happen, and I informed him that I would not be attending church again.

So, at fifteen or so, I left the church and stopped believing in God until approximately 38, which was 1990 approximately.

I was pretty much an atheist up until 1990, when one day my wife saw a murder on the T.V. She was not a Christian and had never been to church except for weddings and funerals, but she went into the bedroom and prayed to God on account of this dreadful murder which was shown fairly explicitly on the T.V. (The thing that affected her was that the people hacking the poor person to death seemed to be enjoying it)

So, unknown to me, my wife had been praying, and a day or so later, we went out to buy a car in a car yard. (We have now moved to Bunbury in Western Australia). Our children were quite small, so I stayed in the car looking after them while she went into the car yard looking at cars.

A guy starts talking to her, and after about half an hour, she returns to the car and announces that this guy is coming around our house to talk to us that evening about God. When he came to our house and started talking to us, I got into an argument with him, so he started quoting the Bible. I say it's just a load of rubbish; he asks if I have read the Bible, and I say no, so he says you read it, then we can discuss it.

He also says that if you read it with your intellect, you'll not understand it; you have to pray to God to give you the ability to understand it. I say, "Look here, mate, you are asking me to pray to a God I don't believe in, to give me the understanding of a book. I think it is a load of rubbish", and he says, "Yes, that's it exactly."

So that night, I knelt by the side of my bed and said a prayer that was not very respectful "Oh

God (If there is one because I don't believe there is), Please give me the understanding to read the bible."

That night I read the Bible for half an hour, the next night a little more, etc. I read the Bible for 4 to 5 hours a night by the end of a week. I used to go to bed, read from 8:00 pm to 1:00 or 2:00 in the morning, and get up to work at 6:30. (I didn't feel tired either)

As I read the Bible, I understood it, but more importantly, I understood one very important fact. Abraham, Isaac, Jacob nearly everyone of any name in the Bible was no different to me; they all had some sin or problem in their life.

Yet God spoke to them; I believed that if God spoke to them, he would speak to me also. And little by little, I learned to hear God speaking to me. Not only could I hear God speaking to me, but I could ask him questions and advice, and he would answer me. Listening to God led me to conflict with church authorities which I shall explain later in the book.

I later understood that the Holy Spirit was speaking to me, but when we are baby Christian, all we need to be concerned about is that if we believe God will speak to us, he will.

Why does that happen?—Simply all spiritual gifts and blessings from God since Jesus came received by faith. If you believe, then it shall be done for you. If you seek, then you shall find.

So how do we hear God speak to us? In my own experience, in the beginning, it was a very quiet voice in my mind. Sometimes it was difficult to decide what was on my mind and what was God. But sometimes, God would speak so clearly that there was no doubt.

Later, when God used to instruct me to do things for him, a great feeling of peace would envelop me, so there was no doubt that it was God.

Do not doubt that God can speak to you, and he will speak to you. Many people fear satan more than they trust God. If God desires to speak to you and the matter is important, he will ensure that you understand. If he does not clearly understand what he is saying, do not be concerned as it is unimportant.

What is important is that you have a personal relationship with Jesus, which requires a two-way conversation; you are talking with God, and God-talk with you. How can you have a personal relationship if only one side talks and the other never replies?

I will cover this aspect in the Chapter on Spending Time with God.

I hope I have not bored you and that you have understood some of the important points of my spiritual journey so far.

Please be patient; I have set the foundation stone that all things are possible if you believe in Jesus; spend time in His presence as a friend, and he will speak to you.

CHAPTER 1

THE VISION

ONE DAY WHILE SITTING in my office at work in 1995 at Millennium Chemicals in Bunbury, Western Australia, it was 9:00 am. I suddenly started to weep and shake from head to foot; I was filled with great fear and became troubled, was I going mad? What was happening?

Suddenly there was a blinding white light; I could no longer see the walls or anything in my office; I was no longer sure I was even in my office.

Suddenly Jesus appeared before me; I was in the presence of the risen glorified Jesus.

White hair, eyes like blazing fire, with a white robe.

He spoke to me and said, "Do not look back at the early church as the Golden Age of the Church; the Golden Age of the Church is just about to start."

I had never read such a thing, so I said, Lord, where in your word does it say this. He said, "I have not stated it specifically but alluded to it in the miracle I performed at the wedding in Cana in Galilee where I turned the water into wine; the master of the feast said most people serve the best wine first, but you have kept the best till now. Therefore, the Golden age of the church is about to start; more and greater miracles and wonders will be performed than were ever performed by my first Church in Jerusalem ".

I said Lord, how will this come about. Jesus said, "I appointed first Apostles, second Prophets, and then Evangelists, pastors, and teachers. The

Priests have usurped the best place for themselves and will not let the others minister".

"I have prepared a great harvest field, the harvest is ready, but the workers are few; I have raised you workers to go into the fields and gather in the harvest, but the priests walk around the outside of the field and will not let the workers go in and gather in the harvest, neither will they go in and gather it themselves. Therefore, I am against the priests who will not let my workers gather in the harvest".

Jesus then went on to say that he was restoring the ministry to lay people and that he would raise the Apostles, Prophets, Evangelists, Pastors, and Teachers he needed and personally appoint them. Those churches that accepted those ministries and allowed them to operate in the church would be blessed, and those churches that would not accept those ministries or allow them to operate would be closed down.

Jesus spoke to me from 9:00 am until 12:30 pm. He told me many things, some I can't remember, others I have not been instructed to reveal at this time.

Immediately after Jesus left, the bright white light receded, and I returned to my office. I was so weak and drained of energy; I went to my boss and asked if I was not feeling well and could I go home. So, I went home and shared these things with my wife. I was still very tired and weak, so I went to bed and slept until the next day.

CHAPTER 2

Spending Time with God

As I said in the introduction, I spent 3 or 4 hours a night reading the Bible over a couple of months.

First, I read the gospels and the New Testament, then started at Genesis and worked my way through the Bible. Over quite some months, I completely read through the Bible about 3 times.

I believed God was speaking to me, and now I was learning to hear his voice better and better.

Now came a time when the Holy Spirit started to tease me gently into spending more time with him early in the morning before I went to work. This started at half an hour a day, then an hour a day, then one and a half hours a day, and then up to 2 hours a day.

So, I would get up at 4:30 in the morning and spend time with God until 6:30, when I had to get ready for work. I want to say that this was not a burden; I looked forward to getting up and spending time in God's presence. The time went very quickly, or so it seemed, and the time for me to go to work came round much too quickly. Getting up and spending time with God was a gift; I did not have to strive to get up.

There are seasons when God will draw you very close to himself and seasons when he feels much further away. When you feel him drawing you, spend as much time in his presence.

So, what did I do when I was spending time with God? This is very easy to answer. The Spirit

of God leads those sons of God; those who worship God must worship him in Spirit and Truth.

This means that at the start of my time with God, I would say wonderful Holy Spirit, what would you like me to do.

Sometimes he would give me teaching from the Bible; sometimes, he would ask me to pray for someone or something. Sometimes he would ask me to sit in silence and meditate on Jesus; other times, he would ask me to worship Jesus.

So how did the Holy Spirit teach me from the Bible? First, he would tell me to turn to a certain scripture, so into my mind would come to the name of the book, chapter, and verse in the Bible. I would turn to it and read it. Then he would give me another one, and I would read it, and so on for 3 or 4 scriptures. Then at the end of reading them, I would have some complete teaching of things I had never heard taught before.

I would like you to understand that the Bible is not just a book; it is a personal love letter from God. To receive the full Blessing from reading it, only God (the Holy Spirit) can give you the understanding and make it a personal message to you.

When Moses is read in the Synagogue, a veil remains over the people. Therefore, God has to remove the veil; when you read that God sent Moses to Egypt to deliver his people, take out Moses' name and replace it with your own. Who is God sending you to so that his people can be delivered? Abraham was a friend of God; God made promises to Abraham. Take Abraham's name out and replace it with your own; God is your friend; what promises is he making to you.

I have often read something that happened to someone in scripture, and I have taken their name out, put it in my own, and said, "Lord, please make this happen to me; please bless me as you have blessed them. It says God is not a respecter of person; if you spend time with God and become his close friend, there is not one promise that God made to someone in the Bible that he will not make to you if you obey him to the same degree as that person."

In praying for people, I would suddenly be given a picture of someone or something in my mind and knew I had to pray for the person or thing. I did not have to think hard about the words I needed to pray because the Holy Spirit gave them to me, and they flowed very naturally.

In waiting on God in silence, you never know what will happen. I encourage you to have patience and persevere; I know that sometimes nothing appears to be happening, but it is, and when something does happen, it is a life-changing experience.

I want you to understand something not taught in churches clearly; you do not have to die and go to Heaven to meet Jesus in person.

Even in the Old Testament, God walked on the earth and spoke to people. Abraham regularly had visits from God. God even stopped and had lunch with Abraham outside his tent. God told him face to face his plans for Abraham and his descendants. God told him of his plans to destroy Sodom and Gomorrah. Abraham even bartered with God and got him to agree that if he found 10 righteous people, he would not destroy Sodom.

And so, you read of Isaac meeting with God, Jacob meeting with God and having a wrestling match. If you read some of the Prophets, Isaiah, Jeremiah, and Daniel, they had amazing encounters with God.

Did this meeting personally with God/Jesus finish in the New Testament of the Bible? I don't think so; even while Paul was persecuting Christians, Jesus appeared to him on the road to Damascus. Jesus appeared to him later in his life, and he was taken up into Heaven in the Spirit. Jesus appeared to the apostle John in person and took him to Heaven.

I am trying to build your faith to receive the Blessing that Jesus can appear in the room with you in person if he wants to. There is no teaching in the Bible that says that this can't happen. I tell you the Truth and am not lying; I have met Jesus many times and been taken to Heaven.

It will if you believe that such a thing can happen to you. Only God will decide the timing. On one occasion, I was sitting in my lounge room praying and worshipping when I noticed the wall around the large window opening starting glowing with bands of blue and gold. The window disappeared, and a golden staircase appeared. On each step of the staircase were two golden animals, one at each end of the step. The incredible thing about the animals was that although I knew they were made of gold, they were alive. Jesus appeared at the bottom of the staircase, held his hand, and said, come.

I went and took his hand, we walked up the staircase, and he showed me around, Heaven. I shared this experience with a good friend of mine, Nick; some short time later, a similar experience happened to him where Jesus came and took him up into Heaven and other beautiful experiences.

On another occasion, Jesus came and held my hand, and I found myself transported to Jerusalem. Still, in the time of Jesus, it was an incredible experience as he showed me around, and I saw many places where Jesus talked and spoke to the people.

I could describe many other beautiful experiences I have had where Jesus has personally visited me, but you have enough to believe this can happen to you, and so it will. You must seek your relationship with Jesus, and as you spend more time in his presence, he will visit you either in person or in the Spirit.

I will touch briefly on worshipping God. As you draw closer to God's presence, you will find that the rules will change. What is permissible for others to do is not permissible for you. This will not be burdensome or constricting but quite the opposite because you have found liberty and freedom in your relationship with Jesus.

Understand that Moses had a deep personal relationship with God but could not enter the promised land because he did not obey God but angrily banged the rock with his staff. That might sound very trivial to us but not when you are in the presence of a Holy God.

Ananias and Sapphira died when they lied at a time when God had drawn close to his people. All I am saying is that as you draw deeper into the presence of God, you will have to change because his Holy nature will not allow those things in his presence.

I know that what I am saying may be strange or hard for some of you, but have you read where God sent Moses back to Egypt to bring the people out, and on the way, the Lord tried to kill Moses? It was only the fact that his wife circumcised their Son and touched Moses with the foreskin that Moses' Life was spared. I believe that what was happening here was that Moses had some besetting sin that he was not willing to deal with, and as the Lord drew closer in Holiness to Moses, that Holiness broke out and tried to kill Moses.

Also, read where David brought the Ark back to Jerusalem, and on the way, Uzzah touched the Ark, and the Lord broke out against Uzzah and killed him.

Therefore, true worship is to obey the Holy Spirit in whatever he commands you to do, no matter how simple or silly it seems. If you obey God, you will be continually worshiping him, which will become very heightened during your time spent with God if you worship him then.

Without the cloud of incense, the high priest could not go into the inner Holy of Holies, where God's presence dwelt. So, the more we worship, the deeper we can go into God's presence, not forgetting that Jesus has opened the way for us by sacrificing his blood.

But God still desires us to worship him in Spirit and Truth.

CHAPTER 3

Being Filled with the Holy Spirit

AFTER SOME TIME, MY wife and I felt led to join an Anglican Church in Bunbury, led by a Priest named Joe Hopkins. Joe was a very loving and genuine person.

My wife and I were very blessed to come under his ministry. This church did allow the operation of the Holy Spirit to a limited extent. At least they acknowledged the Holy Spirit and held healing services once a month where people were healed.

Now the Holy Spirit started telling me that I needed to be filled with the Holy Spirit; I was a little confused as I knew by now that I was speaking to the Holy Spirit, and yet here, he was telling me that I needed to be filled with the Holy Spirit. Although not understanding, I obeyed what he was telling me to do.

The church was holding a Saints Alive Course. This was about a 7th week's duration, and on the 8th week, you were prayed to be filled with the Holy Spirit and speak in tongues. The course was quite good, teaching you the basics of Christianity, the Holy Spirit, and the Gifts of the Holy Spirit.

What I liked most was that for 15 minutes before we started, we worshipped God, singing worship songs out of some books while being led by Joe; that was the best part of the course for me.

When it came close to the 8th week, I wanted to be filled with the Holy Spirit, so I fasted for nearly a week to ensure I would receive the Holy Spirit and speak in Tongues.

On the last night of the course, just before we started, Joe said, "Do not think you can earn the Holy Spirit; God gives him the freedom to you as a gift. But in my heart, I said no, I have fasted and prayed, and surely I shall receive the Gift of the Holy Spirit because I wanted to speak in Tongues."

Anyway, my turn came to be prayed for by two ladies, Val Bartholomew and Ann Frost. They were very kind and considerate until the point where under the guidance of the Holy Spirit, they said, "Have you got any sins you want to repent of? Oh, the Holy Spirit convicted me that before I became a Christian, I was addicted to watching pornography and masturbation and still had ongoing problems in this area. And so, I lied and said no, I do not have anything to repent. And so, they laid hands on me, and I felt a great heat over my head and shoulders. Then they prayed for me to speak in tongues, but I could not. So, after praying a blessing for me, I went back into the room with the others, and then we went home."

I was bitterly disappointed that I did not speak in tongues; satan tried to tell me that there was nothing in it at all, but I said no, I felt the heat, and I believe I have been filled with the Holy Spirit, and I shall speak in Tongues in God's timing.

So, for nearly one week, I prayed continually, Lord, fill me with the Holy Spirit and let me speak in Tongues. About one week later, I was at work and a contractor's hut and started flicking through the pages of a girlie magazine. I threw the magazine down in disgust with myself and thought I would never be filled with the Holy Spirit or speak in tongues if I carried on like this.

It was almost an audible voice that said, "You cannot earn the Gift of the Holy Spirit; I give him to you freely. If you go down to the foreshore this lunch hour and repent of your sins, I will fill you with the Holy Spirit, and you will speak in tongues."

I went to the foreshore in Australind during my Lunch hour. It was about 5 minutes walking from my work, and I got down on my knees; it was quiet and secluded.

I repented of my sins, and then God said good, now speak in Tongues. As I started to speak in Tongues, a great power fell on me and overwhelmed me; I fell sideways off my knees, prone to the floor. Then God started to go through my life and show me the times when he had been with me and blessed me, and as God showed me, I would be filled with great joy and weeping for joy, and then he would show me where I had sinned against him, and I would weep bitter tears of repentance.

And so, I was on like a big roller coaster, sometimes weeping for joy and repentance. When God had finished with me, I thought I had better return to work, thinking I had only been lying on the floor for a few minutes.

When I looked at my watch, I had been lying on the floor for over 2 hours and was very weak and drained from the experience.

I went back to my office and felt unable to work, so I locked my office door and spent the rest of the afternoon weeping and worshipping God until I went home. I had such joy sharing with my family what had happened, but it is difficult to explain your experience to someone else, so I have gone over this experience in great detail and hope you will get a blessing from my sharing it with you.

Note: For those who do not know or have not experienced it, speaking in tongues is a gift of the Holy Spirit where you allow him to use your mouth and tongue, and he speaks through you in his chosen language. It can be the language of angels that no one understands but God, or it can be an earthly language, as on the day of Pentecost when the Apostles who were Galileans stood up and spoke in all different languages to the Jews who had gathered from all different countries for the feast.

I also point out that my Son Alec, my Daughter Jenna and my wife Diane all received their gift of speaking in tongues directly from God without anyone praying for them.

And to encourage youngsters, my Son was 7 when he was filled with the Holy Spirit and spoke in tongues, and my daughter was 9. That happened because they knew they existed and asked God for it. Will he give you a stone if you ask your Father for bread? Ask, and you will receive.

It is worth mentioning that I felt the physical presence of the Holy Spirit from this point on. Sometimes I felt his presence more than other times. If he had instructed me to do something, I felt his presence very strongly; this was felt like heat over the back of my head and shoulders also, sometimes I would feel a weight come over my body; it suddenly felt heavy, and other times waves of peace would flow over me, there was no doubt that now the Holy Spirit dwelt within me. As Jesus said, my Father and I will come and dwell in you.

Is this being filled with the Holy Spirit all there is, or is there more? I believe that being filled with the Holy Spirit is a continual process.

Did not Jesus appear amongst the disciples after his resurrection and breathe on them and say, receive the Holy Spirit. Yet later, they said, "Do not leave Jerusalem but wait for the gift my Father promised which you have heard me speak about. For John, baptized with water, but you will be baptized with the Holy Spirit in a few days. After the Sanhedrin released Peter and John, the people prayed, and the place where they were meeting was shaken. And they were all filled with the Holy Spirit and boldly spoke God's word."

The apostle Paul had hands laid on him by a disciple named Ananias to receive his sight and be filled with the Holy Spirit. Yet later, Paul and Barnabas had hands laid on them by the elders in the Church in Antioch so they could be sent on their way by the Holy Spirit. I wish to encourage you that there are different levels in God's

Kingdom, and God will anoint you as you need to go up to the next level.

How we receive the anointing is simple: we obey the Holy Spirit. He is our teacher, our guide, and our counselor. His job is to lead you to grow into the likeness of Jesus, He will take the things of Jesus and make them known to us; he will make Jesus real.

In the following chapters, I will describe some of the experiences and teachings I have received in my spiritual journey so that you may also receive the same blessings or even greater by faith.

CHAPTER 4

Being Filled with the Spirit of Elijah

In Perth, Western Australia, around 1993, 1994, and 1995, was a series of Seminars given by John Wimber and a team associated with him from the Vineyard Church in America. The Vineyard Church in Perth organized the conferences.

I thank John Wimber, all associated with him, and the organizers of those conferences. Undoubtedly, these had a major impact on my walk with God.

After my first John Wimber Conference, the first night, I was lying in bed at home, worshipping and thanking God for all he had done in these conferences. Great waves of love fell on me while I was lying in bed, and I started shaking, not just me but the whole bed, so my wife woke up. And amid this, God spoke to me and said, I have appointed you to be a Prophet.

He said he had taken a portion of the prophetic anointing on Paul Cain (One of the speakers at the Wimber Conference) and placed it on me. I had never read of such a thing, so the following morning, when I got up, I asked the Holy Spirit to show me where similar things happened in the Bible.

He took me back to the Old Testament, where God took a portion of the anointing on Moses and put it on 50 elders so they could assist Moses. He also took me to the New Testament, where Phillip preached the gospel in Samaria and baptized people. Still, they did not receive the

Holy Spirit until Peter and John prayed for them to receive the Holy Spirit.

Also, he showed me where Peter was sent to Cornelius' House, where a number were gathered; as Peter spoke to them, the Holy Spirit came on all who heard. God had already sent an Angel to Cornelius, he could have filled them with the Holy Spirit then, but that was not his plan. He sent Peter to them and took a portion of the anointing on Peter and put it on them.

And so, I found myself being sent to church leaders and giving them prophecies from God. These church leaders were never happy when I spoke to them as God was correcting them most of the time, and they did not want to hear this. I would say to them, the Lord says. They would say they do not say what the Lord says, but I believe the Lord says.

I asked the Holy Spirit if what they were saying was correct; he said no, I had instructed you to say what the Lord says, and that is what you must do. He said to my search through the Bible;

you will not find one prophet who said I believe the Lord is saying. Also, it says to let each prophecy according to their faith.

So, I told the Holy Spirit, why are these men saying you must say I believe the Lord is saying. He said it is because they are rebelling against God, and they know it. If you say I believe the Lord says, then they can say, as well, this is just your imagination, and therefore we do not have to obey what you are saying. But once you say what the Lord says, and in their hearts, they know that God is saying, they now have a problem—do they change their attitude, or do they knowingly continue their rebellion. I said, "Why does the Holy Spirit do this many times? These people become angry at the words I speak when the words do not seem to be offensive in themselves."

He said it is because you have uncovered secrets that they thought were hidden, now you are a threat to them because you know their dark secrets, and they do not want to change. And so, I found having a Prophetic calling was a very hard and lonely path with no one to teach you but the Holy Spirit.

It was interesting, sometimes even amusing, to watch the attacks from the Church leadership. Just the slightest thing which did not seem right to them, and they accused you of being a false prophet; I did not see anyone accusing them when they made a mistake saying, "Hey, you are a false priest or a false pastor or a false teacher or a false evangelist.", But God is justified by his wisdom.

I encourage all of you who are called to be Prophets not to listen to anyone but the Holy Spirit.

Now about being filled with the Spirit of Elijah. (I bet some of you were wondering when I would get to that.)

I was sent to the Seven Day Adventist Church by the Holy Spirit and spent quite a long time there (15 months at a guess).

After some months, they had an evening with a cine film of the Gospel of Luke by the Genesis Foundation. And so, as I watched this film in the darkness, the Holy Spirit started to speak to me, and I shook, and at the point of the film where John the Baptist appeared, The Holy Spirit said, you too are filled with the Spirit of Elijah like John the Baptist.

And so, the following morning, I spent some more time asking the Holy Spirit about this, as I felt that John the Baptist was Elijah, and there was only one person filled with the Spirit of Elijah.

In scripture, the Holy Spirit showed me that John the Baptist said he was not Elijah and that the Angel told his Father Zachariah that John would go on before the Lord in the Power of Elijah. The Holy Spirit said John the Baptist was not Elijah but filled with the power and Spirit of Elijah.

He then told me that John was not the only one at that time of Jesus who was filled with the Spirit of Elijah. I said I had never read such a thing.

He then explained how Jesus' disciples came to him and said, "Teacher, we saw a man driving out demons in your name, and we told him to stop because he was not one of us." Jesus said, "Don't stop him."

The Holy Spirit repeated that many were filled with the Spirit of Elijah at that time of Jesus to prepare for his coming. Still, John the Baptist was chiefly used, and his name is recorded in the Bible, whereas the other names are recorded in the Lamb's Book of Life. And so, I believed in the Holy Spirit and was filled with the Spirit of Elijah.

I also shared this with my wife, Diane. Some short time later, a lady called Sue Barnes gave a book to her friend Ann Frost who gave it to me. The book was titled "The Elijah Task by John Sandford."

And without reading it, I gave it to my wife and said see, I believed the Holy Spirit about being filled with the Spirit of Elijah, which is what the book is about.

The Holy Spirit fell on me as I spoke, and I prophesied for quite a few minutes but personally did not remember anything I had said. A couple of hours later, my wife, reading the Book the Elijah Task, got very excited and said, "Look, the prophecies you spoke out earlier are written down in this book almost word for word. I do not have a copy of this book as I gave it back, but you can read them for yourself if you buy the book."

I do not specifically remember what is written in the book, but I know it was part of my spiritual journey and a key to receiving the Spirit of Elijah. I thank those who were faithful under the guidance of the Holy Spirit for giving me the book.

I want to encourage people, particularly those God has called, to pray and earnestly desire to be filled with the Spirit of Elijah.

I have given examples of how the Spirit of Elijah is used in Chapter 8, The Works.

CHAPTER 5

BEING BAPTIZED WITH FIRE

ONE DAY, I READ the Bible and the scripture where John the Baptist said I baptize you with water, but one more powerful than I will come, and he will baptize you with the Holy Spirit and with fire. As I read this, I said, "Yes, I have been baptized with the Holy Spirit, and the fire is the Holy Spirit purging me and making me holy."

Almost audibly, the Holy Spirit said, "No, being baptized in the Holy Spirit and fire is two completely separate actions. You can be baptized with the Holy Spirit, and then you can be baptized with fire." I said Holy Spirit, I have never heard of such a thing, but I will believe in what you say.

So, for 10 months, I fasted and prayed Lord to baptize me with the fire of the Holy Spirit.

One evening, after praying for approximately 10 months. My wife and I were praying for all the Churches in Bunbury and the South West, and as we prayed, we were both given a vision looking down over Bunbury and the South West. The whole area was in darkness, and there was a little pinprick of light (minute). And a voice said you are the light that shines in the darkness. Now it was around 9.00 pm.

The following day I went to work; with my friend, Pastor Malcolm Holloway, who came into my office and worked at the same place. He said a strange thing happened last night.

We have a prophet named Bob Anderson from the Assemblies of God Church in Perth staying with us; right in the middle of our evening meal, he looked off into the distance and said you are the light that shines in the dark. The prophet then told them that he saw a vision of great darkness covering the area of the South West with just a little pinprick of light. I said that is incredible; that is exactly the vision my wife and I saw last night; what time did the prophet see this. Malcolm replied that it was around 9,00 o'clock in the evening.

I said that was the same time we were praying. Malcolm said I believe God wants you to come and meet this man. So that evening, I set off to meet at Malcolm and Gaik-Sim Holloway's House in Capel.

When I got there, I was introduced to Bob, and he started sharing some of the things God had sent him to do. Some of the things he was describing were just wonderful, and it was obvious God had anointed him to do some great works.

While I was listening to his testimony, the Holy Spirit said to be bold and ask for whatever you want—thinking back to what happened to me with Paul Cain, how God took the anointing from Moses and put it on others, and how Elisha had asked for a double portion of Elijah's Anointing. I interrupted and said I want a double portion of the anointing on your Life.

Bob was taken aback, smiled, and said, " Let me ask God first. He prayed for a brief space and said, "No, the Holy Spirit has said that what you want is to be baptized with fire." I said, "Yes, please pray for me to be baptized with fire."

So, we stood up, and he prayed for me. I do not remember the words, but I suddenly felt this intense burning feeling. I opened my eyes to see if I could see any fire, but I could not, so I closed them again.

The feeling of fire was pleasant at first, but then it got hotter and hotter. Also, I started shaking from head to foot; I must be honest, and I started to wonder how bad this burning sensation would get.

It exceeded my expectations, and so did the shaking until it got to the point where I thought this was going to kill me. So, I cried out, "Lord, please stay your hand; I think I will die, and my body cannot bear this much power."

And slowly, the burning subsided until I felt hot all over, particularly on the palms of my hands and the center of my forehead. When I opened my eyes, I could see two small flames on my hands, I asked the others if they could see any flames on the palms of my hands, but they said they could not.

I was weak, and the burning sensation was still greatly reduced, so I decided to drive back from Capel to Bunbury. It was very late and dark as I drove along at 110km/hr.

I started thanking God and was led to pray for the Churches in the area. As I was praying, I looked up and saw a bright green star in the sky and thought this was odd. The star was moving and getting closer and getting bigger. I started to feel that this bright green star would hit my car and wondered what was happening. The star was very close now, and it looked like it was going to hit my car, so I jammed on the brakes, and the car speed dropped to around 40 km/hr. The star was about 50 feet in diameter, hit the road about 50 feet in front of me, and disappeared. At the same time, I heard an audible voice say, "I saw satan fall like lightning from heaven." (Luke 10:18)

And so, I got home feeling shaky from the experience and lying in bed; I still had the burning sensation all over, particularly on the palms of my hands and the center of my forehead. (This feeling of all over lasted for a few days and then slowly subsided and disappeared, but the sensations on my hands and forehead would appear many times when I prayed for people.)

And so, I asked the Holy Spirit what the meaning of the burning sensation in the middle of my forehead was. The Holy Spirit told me that it was symbolic that I had been sealed by the King of Kings and Lord of Lords, and I shall not sin anymore.

The following morning the Holy Spirit showed me that scripture in revelations that confirmed I had been sealed. Also, at work that morning, Malcolm Holloway popped his head into my office and said, "I've got a word from the Lord for you—you've been sealed by the King of Kings and Lord of Lords, and you shall sin no more. I said thanks, Malcolm. You are spot on."

So, what is the point of being baptized in fire—all I can tell you is that if you want the Apostolic anointing, you need to be baptized with fire. I believe that our spiritual journey is a series of stages. Some are to be completed on earth, others to be completed in Heaven when we die. But if we understand the journey and the critical stages, we can complete those down here on earth that the majority must complete in Heaven.

Also, we will be able to bless others to a much greater degree because of the stage of our journey, our openness to the Holy Spirit leading, and the power he has given us.

CHAPTER 6

THE KEYS TO THE APOSTOLIC ANOINTING

UNDERSTANDING THE KEYS TO Apostolic Anointing is very easy, and all we have to do is obey the Holy Spirit, who will teach us and lead us through each stage. This also means that we must obey the Holy Spirit and carry out his instructions no matter how simple and trivial they appear. (Please note that I know this is not easy sometimes. I confess there have been times when I have rebelled and deliberately disobeyed the Holy Spirit in my life. Still, I thank God's protection that I have nearly always obeyed the Holy Spirit in God's Kingdom work.)

The keys to Apostolic anointing are mainly written in the lives of Jesus' Disciples as they grew spiritually into Apostles. Some are also principles that have also been present in the Old Testament.

With the help of the Holy Spirit, I will try and make this easier for you to understand. But only from the point of increasing your faith and knowledge so that you ask the Holy Spirit for these things. Jesus says you have not because you ask not, and my people perish for lack of knowledge. If you know and believe these things exist by faith, you can ask the Holy Spirit, who will show you what processes you must go through to obtain these blessings.

Some of these may be obvious, but please be patient.

1. Belief in God
2. Belief in Jesus

3. Jesus is the Father, is the Son, is the Holy Spirit; they are separate and one
4. Meeting the Jesus of Nazareth
5. Meeting the Risen Jesus
6. Meeting the Glorified Jesus

You only need the above to receive Apostolic Anointing. God decides who receives this anointing, but we are encouraged to pray for and ask for this ministry and all spiritual gifts, for God will grant you the desires of your heart if your motive is pure and unselfish.

Other Blessing which you can receive at higher levels or lower levels as God determines.

7. Meeting the Father
8. Meeting the Holy Spirit
9. The Ministry and Spirit of Elijah and Moses
10. Your Personal Key—given to you by the Holy Spirit

How do you know which level your cat is at—close your eyes and start praying to God-who. Do you see—that is your level.

1) Belief in God

This is the first basic step. It doesn't matter if you are a Jew, a Muslim, or a Christian. We believe in worship and praying to the same God. The God of the Jew, the God of the Muslim, and the God of the Christian are the same. The Old Testament of the Christians is the same as the Jewish Torah. The Koran clearly states that Christians, Jews, and Muslims are all brothers and peoples of the scriptures.

The Koran honors Mary as the mother of Jesus, and the Koran even declares that Jesus is the Messiah. (See chapter 8, The Works)

The Jews (Israel) have more right to be called the people of God than the Christians, as God chose that race to be a people unto himself as the line from which the Messiah Jesus would come.

Today, the Christian Church has forgotten that it is just an offshoot of the first Jewish Church in Jerusalem. All the promises in the Bible were made firstly to Jews, and as an aside, God added in the Gentiles if they believed in his Son Jesus.

I write these things so that Christians do not think themselves superior to the Jews or Muslims. God made a covenant with Abraham to bless his descendants through Isaac (the Jews), but he would also bless his descendants through Ishmael (the Muslims). Therefore, God has a special place in his heart for the Jew and Muslims.

If you do what is right, you will be acceptable to God, but there are certain promises that God made to the Nation of Israel that that nation can only fulfill. We, as Christians, have been tacked onto the end of those promises by faith in the name of Jesus.

As Paul said, we have been grafted into the Vine (the Jewish promise), but God can just as easily cut us out again if we do not continue in the faith of Jesus (I am speaking nationally as well as individually here)

Many religions worship God in the old covenant to put things in the right perspective. We as Christians are not any better or superior to them, but because of the new Covenant of Grace, we can expect better promises. And the blessings we receive are received by faith and not by works.

You cannot earn any blessing from God in the New Covenant. (Do not confuse this with God still expecting you to keep yourselves Holy)

I feel that the Holy Spirit is asking me to write these words because many churches feel they are superior when they are not. Read Jesus' words to the churches at the beginning of revelations.

If you believe in God, you are doing well. If you believe in his Son Jesus, you are doing better. In addition to the above—is the Holy Spirit given to Jews and Moslems—yes, he is. I saw a documentary once where Muslims were on a pilgrimage, baptized in water, and the Holy Spirit came on them. (I checked it out with the Holy Spirit, and he said yes, that's me)

Are there Christians, Jews, and Muslims that are not filled with the Holy Spirit –Yes, there are plenty of those religions that do not know God or the Holy Spirit?

2) *Belief in Jesus*

In the first covenant, the Jews had to be kept holy by the Priests offering sacrifices for the people's sins. Once a year, the blood of Lambs and other sacrifices paid the price of the people's sins so they could become holier and draw nearer to God. But even so, the priest was generally kept as an intermediary between God and the people. (There were some exceptions where God bypassed the priests and went directly to the people, but this was not the normal way God operated.)

Even though the price had been paid for their sins, none of the people were allowed to enter the Holy of Holies. Only the priests were allowed to enter the Holy of Holies. After ritual cleansing and offering sacrifices for their sins, they also took an incense to shield themselves from God's presence.

The priests went into the Holy of Holies to minister to God once a year. i.e., once a year, one person in the whole of the Jewish nation was allowed to get up close to God. (the Old Covenant)

With the crucifixion and death of Jesus, he offered himself once and for all as a perfect sacrifice and, by his blood, cleansed all who believed in him from all sins, past, present, and future. His faith enables the believer to go into the Holy of Holies, not in the earthly one that was a copy, but into the Heavenly Holy of Holies.

Therefore, by faith in Jesus, we have obtained the right to go into God›s presence ourselves without requiring a priest or a pastor as an intermediary.

God has opened up the way for us to go into his presence and have a deep personal relationship with him.

Now are Jews and Muslims able to hear and speak to God—Yes, they are. Are they able to enter the Holy of Holies—No, they are not. Only the High Priest once a year can enter the Holy of Holies. God has strict rules and regulations on how the Holy Spirit can operate in the Old Covenant. When Jesus ascended into Heaven, God sent out the Holy Spirit on all flesh, but only those who received Jesus in their hearts would be able to operate in the gifts of the Holy Spirit in the New Covenant.

The Holy Spirit says don't get hung up or confused by this as God is in the process of changing from the old covenant to the new, and some areas will become blurred. Don't forget that the whole nation of Israel will be converted to believe in Jesus in a single day, and this always starts with a remnant going before the rest.

3) Jesus is the Father, the Son, and the Holy Spirit; they are separate and one.

This is the Job of the Holy Spirit to give each person a revelation of the Father, the Son, and the Holy Spirit. The relationship between them is very complicated, and reading the Bible may even appear as if it contradicts itself in some areas.

God has revealed himself progressively to the Jewish nation in encounters or revelations. In the beginning, God did not give his name; sometimes, when he appeared to people and asked his name, he replied, "Why do you want to know?"

But slowly, as the relationship with his people unfolded, God revealed his name and sometimes changed or added to it. In the beginning, his name was the Lord God (Adam in Genesis), or the Lord, or God (Noah in Genesis), (Abraham in Genesis). In Exodus, God calls Himself the God of Abraham, Isaac, and Jacob (Moses in Exodus). (To explain that he was the God who would fulfill the covenant he had made with Abraham, Isaac, and Jacob)

Moses was persistent and said yes, but if I say the God of my fathers has sent me to you, they ask, "What is his name?" Then what shall I tell them? God answers, I AM who I AM; you are to say to them I AM sent me to you.

When the people are brought out of Egypt, they continue to murmur against God, and God gets a bit annoyed about it and goes back to using his title of the Lord God. But to those who find favor, Moses Aaron, Nadab and Abihu, and Seventy Elders of Israel went up Mount Sinai and saw the God of Israel, and God did not raise his hand against those elders of Israel; they saw God, and they ate and drank in his presence. But to Moses, who finds even greater favor, Moses asks God to see His Glory.

He told Moses he would grant his request, but no man may look at his face and live.

He causes all his goodness to pass in front of Moses, but Moses is covered by his hand and removes his hand so Moses can see his back. Then the Lord proclaims it is named. "The Lord, the compassionate and gracious God, slow to anger, abounding in love and faithfulness, maintaining love to thousands, and forgiving wickedness, rebellion, and sin. Yet he does not leave the guilty unpunished. He punishes the children and their children for the fathers› sin up to the third and fourth generation."

I do not want to dwell on this subject longer as it is such a large subject that it could fill a book to say that the revelation of God's nature and the name was continued through the books of the prophets. He gave his name as Father, the comforter, the provider, the God who heals, the redeemer, and the savior.

We now come closer to the present when John the Baptist prepared the way for the coming of Jesus by proclaiming repentance and baptism in water for the forgiveness of sins.

At the coming of Jesus, we have entered the new covenant where he uses his name, the God who saves—Jesus the Christ—the anointed one.

Before Jesus appeared on the earth, his coming was prophesied, and his nature was expounded in all its facets. As prophesied by Isaiah, "For to us a child is born, to a son is given, and the government will be upon his shoulders, and he will be called Wonderful, Counselor, Mighty God, Everlasting Father, Prince of Peace, of the increase of his government and peace there will be no end."

Therefore, Jesus is fulfilling God›s revelation of his nature and name. Jesus said it was his Father›s name and the name of the Holy Spirit. Before he was taken into heaven, he told his followers, "All authority in heaven and earth has been given to me. Therefore, make disciples of all nations, baptizing them in the name of the Father, Son, and the Holy Spirit."

4) Meeting the Jesus of Nazareth

Once you have believed in God, you can meet Jesus of Nazareth. Just as the fisherman of Galilee met Jesus in person, that opportunity is available today. As Jesus lived amongst them, his first objective was to reveal the love of the Father to them and make known the Father's Character.

He also taught them, and they grew spiritually. As we grow spiritually, we are given a greater understanding and asked to make choices. Sometimes we do not understand what the Holy Spirit is saying, but he still expects us to choose for or against what he tells us.

Jesus' disciples came to tricky teaching where Jesus said unless you eat my flesh and drink my blood, you have no life. After this teaching, many of his disciples returned and no longer followed him.

I want to encourage you that the Holy Spirit has often told me things I did not understand, but I have believed or acted on those things. And later, I received a massive blessing, teaching, or revelation because of my faith. In the new covenant, we receive things by faith (not because our brain understands).

In this level of Jesus of Nazareth, you will be given limited power and authority. Jesus sent the twelve to preach the good news and perform signs, wonders, and healings. He also sent out seventy-two to prepare the way where he was going.

So, expect God to use you even at the lower levels. God will never send you to do anything greater than your faith level. But also understand that his purpose is to make you grow spiritually. Therefore, you will be asked to do things where you may think you are out of your depth. If you remember that the Holy Spirit is doing the work and you are just the vessel he is working through, you should not have any problems.

When God feels you are ready, he will move you to the next level; you will know you have moved levels, which will be quite a significant jump.

5) Meeting the Risen Jesus

With the Jesus of Nazareth level, I told you to believe things the Holy Spirit told you, even if you did not understand them. If you remember, when Jesus was with the disciples, he told them many things, but they did not understand, and the meaning was hidden. But after Jesus was crucified and rose from the dead, they understood many things he said. (But there were some things he said which we are still waiting to see fulfilled—i.e., you will have to go through some more spiritual growth to understand)

At this level, the Holy Spirit will reveal the risen Jesus. You will be given a greater revelation and love of what Jesus has done for us. I don›t think anyone on this earth who fully understands what Jesus accomplished for us by his crucifixion, death, and resurrection. Even the apostle Paul said he did not have the full revelation and received his gospel revelation directly from heaven.

We often read or hear of God's promise or teaching to us, but it is just a superficial or surface understanding. I remember I had a tape of Christian music, one of the songs was about the crucifixion of Jesus; I had heard it many times. But after the revelation of the Risen Jesus, I wept with great grief and also Joy. Grief for the terrible suffering that Jesus went through and Joy for the blessings I had received because of his sacrifice.

I do not want to dwell too much on the teachings you will receive at each level, as the Holy Spirit will deal with each person as he feels appropriate. I want to explain that these levels do exist, and you need to try and grow spiritually by faith and attain these levels, which are milestones in your spiritual growth.

As the Holy Spirit gives you a greater revelation of the Risen Jesus, you will be given greater spiritual power and asked to do larger tasks for God. (All anointed workers for God have gone through this process, some may not have realized it because the Holy Spirit may have lumped some of the stages together.)

He will take you to the next level when you have accomplished all the changes in your life and understood what the Holy Spirit is teaching you. His purpose is to transform you into the likeness and character of Jesus and make you Holy so you can endure being in the presence of his Glory.

6) Meeting the Glorified Jesus

Those who think Jesus is some puny lamb wandering around heaven bleating are shocked. When the glorified Jesus turns up, people fall at his feet like dead men, sometimes in great fear and terror. I feel sorry for the people who ridicule, revile, hate Jesus, and treat him with contempt; they will be terrified by his awesome presence when he shows up. We must go through the previous stages to prepare ourselves for such an ordeal.

When the apostle John met the Glorified Jesus, he had been a close friend of the Jesus of

Nazareth, but what happened. John says I fell at his feet as though dead when I saw him. Then he placed his right hand on me and said, "Do not be afraid. I am the first and the last. I am the living one; I was dead and am alive forever and ever. And I hold the keys of death and Hades."

Let me issue a warning here if you do not have real love in your heart for Jesus, and you are doing this to get spiritual power, and you do not have genuine respect and reverence for the Son of God, you are in big trouble when you get to this level.

No longer is Jesus meek and mild, "I saw heaven standing open, and there before I was a white horse, whose rider is Faithful and True. With Justice, he rides out and makes war. His eyes are like blazing fire, and many crowns on his head. He has a name written on him that no one knows. He is dressed in a robe dipped in blood, and his name is the Word of God; the armies of heaven were following him, riding white horses and dressed in fine linen, white and clean. Out of his mouth comes a sharp sword to strike down the nations. He will rule them with an iron scepter. He treads the winepress of the fury of the wrath of God Almighty. He has this name written on his robe and thigh: King of Kings and Lord of Lords."

The revelation the Holy Spirit gives us at this level is that we are warriors, and he has empowered us to carry out warfare against the enemy's works. He has given us power and authority to defeat the enemy's works, but understand it is his power we are using, and we still have to obey his instructions.

The average Christian will go through the levels above before they die and go to heaven. Levels 7 and 8 will be achieved by those who are keen, dedicated, and willing to pay the price.

7) Meeting the father

You cannot meet the Father unless you know Jesus.

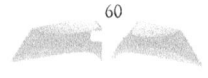

Jesus said, "I am the way, the Truth, and the Lifeline. No one comes to the Father except through me." One time, Jesus showed me around heaven when he showed me a huge door: "This is the door to God the Father›s Throne Room. "May I go in?" I asked.

I think Jesus wanted me to go somewhere else, but he could see I wanted to go in. So, the door opened, and Jesus, holding my hand, let go. "Are you not coming in as well?" I asked. "No," he said, you have to meet the Father on your own.

So, I walked into the room, and in the middle was a throne, but I was approaching the back of the throne. God the Father was standing with his back to me, He started speaking to me (I can›t remember what he said), and during the conversation, I started thinking about what it would be like to look at his face, and I felt I could ask, so I said: "Can I look on your face?". He laughed quietly and said, "No man can look on my face and live; if you look on my face, you cannot go back to the world but must stay here forever."

I understood what he was offering me. I started thinking about my wife, my Son, and my Daughter and what would happen to them if I did not return. As I was about to say, I think it would be better if I went back. In an instant, I was transported back to my house.

I have often conversed with people and Christians and asked, "Do you believe in God?" To their surprise, I say, "No, I do not believe in God."

Belief is hope for some future event. God is a fact, a 100% certainty without any doubt. That's the benefit of revelation, and it increases your faith and removes doubt and fear.

8) Meeting the Holy Spirit

The Holy Spirit is the Glory of God. You cannot approach him as you can, the Son of God. Jesus said anyone who sins against the Son of man would be forgiven, but whoever sins. (Blasphemes) against the Holy Spirit will never be forgiven. You will know God is present when the Glory comes (which can be manifested as Apostolic Anointing). You will display great reverence and fear; I am not talking just in church. All the people held the Apostles in great respect and were afraid to join them.

Also, great judgment will fall if you sin against the Holy Spirit, Ananias and Sapphira fell dead because they lied to God in the presence of the Holy Spirit (Glory). The apostle Paul cursed someone opposing him, and he was struck blind.

I must be perfectly honest; I have not gotten into this level yet, I started to enter, and then the Holy Spirit said that I could not fully enter this level because I was unwilling to deal with certain issues in my life yet.

The problem of trying to enter this level without dealing with outstanding issues can have dire consequences. (See where the Lord instructed Moses to go to Egypt and then tried to kill him on the way.) Also, the Lord broke out against Uzziah when he put his hand out to steady the Ark.

Suppose you read the whole of Leviticus 10 about the death of Aarons' sons when they offered unauthorized fire before the Lord. Moses also explained to Aaron and his remaining sons how important it was to approach the Lord with the right attitude. (Understand the Glory of the Lord had now come down and was in residence)

I have seen the Holy Spirit, and he is a being completely covered in flame. Some people have met the Holy Spirit if you read. Rees Howells Intercessor, Benny Hinn Good Morning Holy Spirit, Smith Wigglesworth - I do not remember the Book Title. And I am sure there are many others.

I am making you aware that you can meet the Holy Spirit as long as your heart is right and he invites you into his presence. Just ask him what you need to do to obtain this Blessing.

9) The Ministry and Spirit of Elijah and Moses

God has two prophetic ministries by which he accomplishes many works. The Spirit of Elijah is a prophetic ministry of restoring love and relationships, and the Spirit of Moses is a prophetic ministry restoring Holiness. These are the two central ministries and anointings God uses.

When Jesus took Peter, James, and John up a high mountain by themselves, he was transfigured before them. Two men, Moses and Elijah, appeared in glorious splendor, talking with Jesus. They spoke about his departure, which he was about to bring to fulfillment at Jerusalem.

God shows that Moses and Elijah are part of Jesus' work and ministry. The Book of Revelation says, I will give power to my two witnesses, and they will prophesy for 1,260 days, clothed in sackcloth. These are the two olive trees and the two lampstands that stand before the Lord of all the earth. Fire comes from their mouths if anyone tries to harm them and devours their enemies. This is how anyone who wants to harm them must die.

These men have the power to shut up the sky so that it will not rain when they are prophesying, and they have the power to turn the waters into blood and strike the earth with every kind of plague as often as they want. (The same powers that Moses and Elijah were given). This scripture also fulfills what was spoken in Zechariah (regarding Zerubbabel).

Zechariah said, "I see a solid gold lampstand with a bowl at the top and seven lights on it, with seven channels to the lights. Also, there are two olive trees, one on the right and one on the left."

"What are these, my Lord?" The Angel replies, "Not by might, nor by power, but by my spirit," says the Lord Almighty.

Later Zechariah repeats the question, "What are these two olive trees on the right and left of the lampstand?" The Angel replies, "These are the two who are anointed to serve the Lord."

Those of you with a Prophetic calling understand what you have been given. Revelations say that the Testimony of Jesus is the Spirit of prophecy, and this gift of prophecy is manifested through the anointing of Moses and Elijah.

Now you need to ask the Holy Spirit for the revelation of these anointings.

10) Your Personal Key—given to you by the Holy Spirit

The Holy Spirit will give you your key to be immediately transported into his presence (or anointed). As your spiritual journey progresses, the key may change. I can only remember three keys.

The first I remember was when John White, at a Wimber Conference, prayed for us, I had never seen a corporate move of the Holy Spirit like that before; the Holy Spirit hit me with some force that nearly knocked me over and then came in waves that also nearly knocked me over and rocked me back and fore as I was standing.

But forgetting the physical manifestation, I was filled with such waves of love and a deep love for the Holy Spirit and Jesus. Whenever I thought back to this time, I would be immediately anointed in the same manner.

The second was after I was baptized with fire, as I prayed for someone and felt the palms of my hands and my forehead burn; if I thought back to that night when I was prayed for, the anointing immediately got stronger.

Although I did not go into great detail, when I entered the throne room of God the Father, it was an awesome experience. The Holy Spirit has given me a mental image of a Golden Key with Jesus written where the part of a key is inserted into a lock.

I walk up to the Throne room of God, insert the key in the door's lock, open the door, and enter the throne room of God, the Father. I am immediately anointed and empowered when I think back on this.

Now I shared the concept that the Holy Spirit will give you your key to be able to enter his presence with a group of Christians I worked with; we used to meet at lunchtime once a week.

A lady named Alice Handley came back with a lovely testimony a week later, where she explained that on her bedroom wall was a picture that her mum had left her. In the picture was a lady wrapped in a cloak. As Alice looked at the picture, the Holy Spirit gave her the impression of imagining herself being wrapped in a cloak as the lady in the picture was.

As she did this, the Holy Spirit came and wrapped himself around her with his presence, and she had the most beautiful encounter with God. This was her key.

I have deliberately not given you too much information about these experiences in this last chapter, and I am making you aware that these things exist so you can desire them and ask for them. The Holy Spirit himself will give you the revelation of each level. But if you have a map, it is easier to find your way. Some of you, the Holy Spirit, may lead differently from the path I have followed.

What is important is that the Holy Spirit prompts us, and we listen to and obey that prompting. Do not be concerned if you hear a sermon where someone says it's OK to do something, but the Holy Spirit says that's not OK for you. It's only because you are on a different level to that person.

CHAPTER 7

The Gifts of the Holy Spirit

THE GIFTS OF THE Holy Spirit are available to everyone. You have to realize that they are gifts, and Jesus gives them to whoever he wants. The power that operates with the gift is directly linked with your relationship with Jesus and is not linked to your goodness or lack of sin. You cannot earn any spiritual gift; you can desire spiritual gifts and pray to receive them.

The main key to operating the gifts is how well you listen to the Holy Spirit and your faith to carry out and believe what he is telling you.

There is no doubt that you feel more anointed sometimes rather than others. But again, I believe this is dependent on our relationship.

If you have stopped spending time with God and your love for him has gone colder than it was, then the anointing of the Holy Spirit on you will decrease. (He will also give you fewer instructions or things to do.) If you spend a lot of time in God's presence and your relationship with him is close and loving, the anointing will be strong.

The most important gift you can have is listening to the Holy Spirit. No matter what gift you have, if the Holy Spirit is not instructing you how to use it, you have become a white witch or warlock. What you are doing is using God's power for your purpose.

Sometimes even in the church, Christians use it to control others and destroy their ministries if they do not submit to the control being exerted.

I want to explain that God's power is neither good nor bad; it is like electricity; what is important is, are we using it for God's Glory, or are we using it for our Glory. Even Satan is using God's power; the difference is that when he or his kingdom comes into contact with someone who is surrendered and led by the Holy Spirit, then that Christian has access to the greater power, or they are a better conduit for the power to flow.

I said earlier that we are to desire spiritual gifts, and you could not desire something if you did not know it existed. There are more gifts than the list given by the apostle Paul. Many Christians have a lack of foresight when they complain or call occult new age gifts, but do not understand there is nothing that the occult has which is not given by God. (They are not using the gift under subjection to God)

Therefore, there is an equivalent Holy Spirit Gift for every new age or occult gift. (Same Power—Same Gifts)

I will make a list of the Gifts (as the Holy Spirit instructs me, and I am sure there are many more that I don't know about) so that you will desire them and pray for them.

1. Prophecy
2. Revelation
3. Visions
4. Speaking in tongues
5. Praying in the spirit
6. Travelling in the spirit
7. Translation
8. Transfiguration into Glory
9. Healings and Miracles
10. Deliverance

1) Prophecy

This gift is the most common gift that the Holy Spirit uses. If you have this gift, do not automatically assume that you have been given the ministry of a Prophet.

Prophecy is a foretelling of the future or speaking a word from God. You do not have to be speaking some amazing future prediction using the prophetic gift, and it can be as simple as the Holy Spirit saying go up to that person and say "God loves you" or something similar.

In ministering to others, when God tells us something unusual about them that only God could know, we call it a word of knowledge, but in fact, you are using the gift of prophecy. This gift is the simplest to operate; you pray and ask the Holy Spirit to come in the name of Jesus and operate the gift in you. You then listen to the small voice speaking in your mind and repeat it word for word.

There is nothing sinful in practicing this gift. If you meet in a little home group or church, put someone in the center and gather around them in a circle. Pray and ask the Holy Spirit to come as above. Then he will give each of you something to say to the person in the middle. Sometimes, what you have been given does not make sense but can profoundly affect the person in the middle. I give examples of this in Chapter 8, The Works, and Chapter 10, Persecution.

I give some advice on operating this gift. If the gift of prophecy comes to you when you are not expecting it, ask the Holy Spirit why he has given it to you. Is the message for you? Are you to pray about it for someone, or are you to go and speak to someone, or are you to speak it out in the church? Also, check when he wants you to speak it out.

It is most important that you ask the Holy Spirit when he wants you to speak and do not speak until he instructs you.

I tell you as a warning of my experience where I believed I had a prophecy for a Church, so I went along, and I kept asking the Holy Spirit when he wanted me to speak, he said not now, and this question and answer went on until the service finished. So, after everyone had left, I quietly sat with the Holy Spirit and said, "Please explain to me what happened here, I believed you sent me here with a prophecy, but I didn't get to speak it."

Eventually, the Holy Spirit said I didn't give you the prophecy or send you here. You had the prophecy from your Spirit and came because you were angry with the church; your obedience when I told you not to speak saved you from making an idiot of yourself.

I beg you not to ignore or overrule the Holy Spirit when you are on God's business.

2) Revelation

Revelation is a gift where God reveals teaching or knowledge to you by the Holy Spirit, which you have never heard before from anyone.

This gift can operate in several ways; it can operate simultaneously through the prophetic gift, the gift of the vision, or both.

In Chapter 2, Spending time with God, I shared how the Holy Spirit would give me teaching (or revelation) by telling me to read several scriptures one after the other. From those particular scriptures would come teaching I had never heard before.

The first thing that happens when you get a revelation like that is satan comes along and says that teaching is not from God, or he gets some other Christian or church leader to say that's not from God.

Scripture tells me that a double-minded man will receive nothing from God. If the Holy Spirit gives you revelation and lets someone persuade you that it's not God, you will grieve the Holy Spirit, and he will eventually withdraw from you.

I want to share how a revelation can be given in a vision, my Daughter Jenna was around 9 years old, and she had a vision where God gave her a gift that was wrapped up.

She undid the wrapping, and there was a box; she opened the box, and inside was a little tongue. She picked the tongue out of the box (in the vision) and put it in her mouth, and immediately she could speak on her tongue.

God gives many revelations to people like that, but they do not understand and think it is their minds.

3) Visions

There are many types of visions which include partial visions (imagination). A true vision is where you have your eyes open, but instead of seeing the normal view, the view you see is the revelation or vision God wants you to see.

You are impervious to things happening around you in the full vision state. The wave patterns of your mind are altered, and you enter almost a trance-like state.

I saw a T.V. program once to prove that a woman had a vision from God; they stuck a needle in her eyeball while she had the vision.

She did not even flinch or blink. The doctor agreed that this had to be supernatural because no one could survive the ordeal of having a needle inserted in their eyeball without flinching or blinking.

So, we can have a vision if God wants to speak to us or show us something. In Joel, God promises to pour out the Holy Spirit on all people, our sons and daughters will prophesy, our old men shall dream, and our young men will see visions.

There are visions from God where he only activates the imagination in our minds. This is normally when he is telling us something personal. Full-blown visions are mostly for some corporate body sharing or some worldwide event.

There is another type of vision described as letting the eyes of your heart be enlightened. The Holy Spirit told me that my heart is not just an organ for pumping blood. When I lower the center of my consciousness to that area of the heart, I feel the anointing and the associated power increase. There are areas in our bodies where the power is concentrated, the palms of our hands are one, and the heart is another.

I know that love is an actual physical force, and this gift is related to that force of love. Please remember that my purpose is to encourage you to seek the Holy Spirit and these gifts, not explain them to you. He will give you the revelation of what it is and how to use it.

When I have been led to pray by the Holy Spirit, sometimes I have been led to pray in a vision and see what I am praying for. I will explain this under item 5. I have prayed for many people to receive the gift of visions, and they assure me that later they did have visions (if not immediately in some cases)

Dreams are just visions when we are asleep; like our imagination, dreams are often not from God. However, if the dream is really important, God will ensure you understand it from him. We must trust his ability to speak to us, not our ability to listen.

Do not forget to pray and check these things with the Holy Spirit.

4) Speaking in tongues

This gift can be given by the Holy Spirit directly or by someone laying hands on you. I know this is an exceptional gift, and I do not believe the Church or Christians understand what they can do with this gift. (Refer to item 10 deliverance)

This gift is unusual because when I pray for the gifts of the Spirit for people, I do not feel much power present. But when I pray for people to speak in tongues, just before they do, I feel a massive surge of power build in my chest and flow down my arms into the person, and then they speak in tongues. That is one of the reasons I think this gift is very important and underused.

Paul said we do not neglect to speak in tongues. One use of this gift is that it builds up your faith if you pray in tongues regularly. Also, when in prayer ministry, it connects you closer to the Holy Spirit. Sometimes, if there seems to be some blockage that the prayer ministry cannot continue, speaking in tongues quietly under your breath sometimes breaks through and gives you the key to completing the ministry. (The Holy Spirit may then give you a word of knowledge or a picture)

When the Holy Spirit asks you to pray, he will ask you to speak in tongues. Do not leave your mind blank but worship God while speaking in tongues.

Finally, to explain why I say we do not fully understand the power associated with the gift of speaking in tongues, I was taking my dog for a walk in the bush behind where I lived in Bunbury, W.A., I came across a Kangaroo (Wallaby) lying on the ground. As we approached the Kangaroo, it jumped up and tried to hop off but immediately fell onto its side.

It could not hop and has damaged itself. I was concerned that if the Kangaroo were left there, it would be set on by a pack of dogs, and also, it was suffering.

So, I tied my dog to a tree and went over to the Kangaroo to pick it up, put it over my shoulder, and carry it back to my house. As I bent down to pick it up, it bit me on the shoulder and scratched me simultaneously.

This was going to be trickier than I thought. Suddenly the Holy Spirit said, try speaking in tongues to the Kangaroo. So, I started speaking in tongues and cautiously bent down to pick up the Kangaroo. This time it was completely calm and allowed me to pick it up and put it over my shoulder.

I continued speaking in tongues, carried it back to my house, and put it in the shade of my chicken pen. I went back and got the dog and then went to call my wife.

She belonged to a group called FAUNA which cared for injured wildlife, she put out her hand to try and touch the Kangaroo, but it tried to bite her. I said try speaking in tongues; she thought I was joking; I said how do you think I got it here, so she spoke in tongues and was able to examine the Kangaroo while it lay perfectly quiet. She said this looks very bad. It might be broken at the hip; let's take it to the Vets. A vet called McGregor; gave his services free to wildlife, so speaking in tongues, I put the Kangaroo in the back of our 4-wheel drive and took it to the Vet.

Speaking in tongues, I carried the Kangaroo to the Vet and put it on the examination table. The Kangaroo had been very calm and quiet all this time; as soon as the Vet touched the Kangaroo, it went ballistic, thrashing around and trying to bite him. In all fairness to the Vet, he knew how to handle the Kangaroo and soon had it under control. But I could see a puzzled look on his face as he asked himself how these people got this thing here.

Unfortunately, the Kangaroo had broken the hip socket and his leg; the Vet said he would never recover from such an injury, and the Kangaroo was mercifully put to sleep.

5) *Praying in the spirit*

Praying in the Spirit is rarely spoken about how it came about for me as I was in a church healing team, and we were about to carry out a ministry for someone.

The priest asked me to speak in tongues, and I didn't quite catch what he said, so I asked him to repeat it. He misunderstood my question and said you know, pray in the Spirit.

Immediately the Holy Spirit said to me Speaking in Tongues and Praying in the Spirit are two different things. So, I started asking people what the difference between speaking in tongues and praying in the Spirit was—nobody knew. And so, over time, I asked the Holy Spirit about this and prayed for the gift.

I was driving down the road at 80km/hr. And was talking to the Holy Spirit, and suddenly he said I would show you what it is like when you pray in the Spirit. I was immediately transported into another realm full of blinding white light.

"I could no longer see the inside of my car or the road." I said, "Holy Spirit, I am driving along at 80 km/hr.", He said, "Don't you trust me." I said, but there was a 90-degree bend ahead; he said, " Don't you think I can steer around corners.

I chickened out and put my foot on the brakes; slowly, the white light disappeared, and I could see the road. I am trying to say that you are transported into Glory when you pray in the Spirit.

Your being becomes one with God. You are no longer praying with words but with emotions and feelings. Words are no longer adequate. Sometimes you are given a vision of what you are praying for. You have raised a prince with God and given authority to govern with him through the prayers he is giving you.

6) Travelling in the spirit

This gift is made much of in the new age, but it is a gift of the Holy Spirit. Jesus used this Gift when

Nathanael came to him; Jesus said to Nathanael, "Here is a true Israelite in whom there is nothing false. "Nathanael said how do you know me. Jesus said, "I saw you while you were under the fig tree before Phillip called you."

Elisha used this gift to enter the same chamber of the King of Aram and then tell the King of Israel all his battle plans. The Holy Spirit allows travel in the Spirit and into the spirit realm. There is no front, back, up, down, space, or time in the spirit realm. You can be instantly transported anywhere and anytime in the blink of an eye.

I want to encourage you that if you believe this gift exists, the Holy Spirit will show you how to use it and go places. Sometimes you will be accompanied. I remember Jesus took me once and showed me around the Holy Land at the time of Jesus. I saw Jesus disputing with the men who brought a woman to him that had been taken in Adultery.

7) Seeing in the Spirit

The kingdom of Heaven is all around us, and we do not have the spiritual eyes to see it. Elisha and his servant were surrounded by troops of the King of Haram (He got fed up with Elisha telling the King of Israel his battle plans). Elisha's servant was afraid.

Elisha told him not to be afraid, as those with us are more than those with them. Elisha prayed, "Oh Lord, open his eyes so he may see. "Then the Lord opened the servant's eyes and saw the hills full of horses and chariots of fire all around Elisha.

Understand that this earth occupies the same space as one of the levels of Heaven. We cannot see it with our earthly eyes. Just a hint, Jesus said to the thief, "today you will be with me in Paradise," and then later instantly materialized in the room with the disciples.

I have often seen angels in churches and the presence of the Holy Spirit. Still, asking others if they had noticed anything unusual, I realized that not many others had seen anything.

8) Translation

I have experienced this gift several times, being physically taken somewhere. In Ezekiel, he was praying near the Kebar River. He had a vision, Then the Spirit lifted him, and he came to the exiles in Tel Abib (Also close to the Kebar River).

The Holy Spirit sent Phillip to speak to an Ethiopian Eunuch in a carriage. He listened to what Phillip had to say and wanted to be baptized. After Phillip baptized him when they came up out of the water, the Spirit of the Lord suddenly took Phillip away, and the Eunuch did not see him again; Phillip, however, appeared at Azotus and traveled about preaching the gospel.

I read a book about Smith Wigglesworth where he was with a group praying in his house; a man from his village came up and knocked on the door and asked them to come and pray for his daughter as she was dying (or dead)

As they all rushed out of the house, Smith Wigglesworth disappeared. The rest of them ran to the man's house and found by asking others; Smith Wigglesworth arrived at the house a full ten minutes before them.

Once I attended a Christian conference in Perth to drive back to Bunbury, a full 2-hour drive. As I left Perth after driving for 15 or 20 minutes, I started to fall into a trance; as I looked at the road through my windscreen, it started going faster and faster in my vision until it became a blur. After what appeared seconds, I found myself still on the main road, but at the turnoff to my house in Bunbury.

I know the journey only took seconds, but when I looked at my watch, a full two hours had elapsed from when I left Perth. The biggest problem with this gift is what happens if the Holy Spirit takes you somewhere and you can't get back.

Therefore, I suggest you keep your passport in your pocket just in case. (Just joking)

9) Transfiguration into Glory

This gift is similar to praying in the Spirit; when you spend time in the presence of God, you will be transformed into his likeness, and His Glory will be manifested on you.

Moses' face glowed; people did not like to see it, and Moses had to cover his face to hide God's Glory. This was the Glory that God would give him in Heaven, manifesting itself before time on the earth. When Jesus was transfigured on the mountain, both Moses and Elijah displayed the Glory that God had given them. When Christians meet the Glory of God, they will be transfigured to a degree into the likeness of Jesus, just as Moses and Elijah were also transfigured at that meeting with Jesus.

10) Healings and Miracles

Every Christian has been given the power for healing under one condition. Only God can give you the authority to use that power. If you listen to the Holy Spirit and obey him, the person will be healed. If you do not listen to the Holy Spirit and pray for someone, they might not be healed.

Don't forget Jesus could not perform many miracles or healings in Nazareth because of their unbelief. It says virtue flowed out of him, and they healed many people. Even early in our spiritual walk, God used my wife and me in an Anglican Ministry Team to pray for people, and God healed them. Refer to Chapter 8, the works.

Note that you must have faith and believe in healing and miracles before seeing them. If you don't believe in this gift, you will not see any healings or miracles done by someone else.

11) *Deliverance*

Deliverance is a gift of the Holy Spirit. Some people have a very strong deliverance of gifting, and this gift enables you to command evil spirits and demons to come out of people.

I witnessed at a John Wimber Conference, where John spoke normally; nothing unusual happened. Then John said, don't be afraid, the Lord has told me a spirit of deliverance will sweep through the place and deliver some of the people.

Things were very quiet for a few minutes, and then people started screaming out, and evil spirits came out of people. Very close to me was a young lady, and as she screamed and the evil Spirit came out of her, she took off, went up into the air, and landed two rows back and 5 chairs along from where she started. Even though she came down from a crash, she did not appear hurt.

I emphasize that this is not something someone told me about; I witnessed it. We have the authority to deliver ourselves; he will tell us if you ask the Holy Spirit what evil spirits or demons we have in us. You can deliver yourself (with the Holy Spirits' guidance) if you repent of the sin that allowed the spirit access, speak in Tongues, and command the Spirit by name to leave in the name of Jesus (in your mind at the same time as you are speaking in tongues).

Just be aware that the evil Spirit or demon will try and trick you, he will try and make you feel sick so that you stop, or you may feel ill or in pain. Ignore this and keep on going, and he has to leave. If the Spirit has a deep hold on you, this process can take 15 or 20 minutes. It is good to fast beforehand to listen to the Holy Spirit better. (Jesus said some kind only come out by prayer and fasting)

Some spirits come out with no manifestation. You will get great peace over you; ask the Holy Spirit, and he will confirm if it's left. (Check in the name of Jesus in case it is a lying spirit trying to imitate the Holy Spirit)

If the Spirit leaves with a manifestation, this can be coughing or retching; there will be no doubt that it has left.

Most importantly, ask the Holy Spirit to come and fill the left space.

CHAPTER 8

THE WORKS

THIS SECTION SHOWS THAT I am an ordinary person, a nobody, but just because I have spent time with God and listened and obeyed the Holy Spirit, he has sent me (and my wife) to do marvelous things.

I want to share how important it is to listen to the prompting of the Holy Spirit.

One day my wife was working in the kitchen, and suddenly the Holy Spirit said (in her mind) go and stand outside on the edge of the road. She thought this was very strange, and again, even more urgently, the Holy Spirit said go and stand outside on the edge of the road. So, she went outside and stood on the pavement at the road's edge. After a few moments, a car came down the hill, going much too fast for a housing estate. And from our neighbor's house across the road came our two children, who were about 8 and 10 at the time. They ran down the neighbor's drive, intending to run straight across the road without looking or stopping. My wife shouted Stop! Stop! They just managed to stop at the pavement's edge as the car passed.

Undoubtedly, if the Holy Spirit had not instructed my wife to stand there, they would have been run over and killed.

When we went to the Anglican Church, it had a healing service once a month. On Sunday, a lady came in using a walking frame and walking in great pain.

We prayed with her for Leukemia and a broken hip; she left the church without her walking frame and in very little pain. A couple of months later, my wife bumped into her while visiting someone in hospital; she was also visiting someone. She told my wife that after we had prayed for her, she returned to her doctor, who sent her for an X-ray. The X-ray showed that her hip had completely knitted together, and the break had healed.

Her doctor was surprised as, when you have Leukemia, any break in a bone forms a chalk line, and it will not grow or heal. So, the doctor wrote her case up in the West Australian Medical Journal as the only person to be healed with a broken bone while suffering from Leukemia.

I apologize for not remembering the lady's name; I only met her once, and my wife met her twice.

Many people were healed in healing services in Anglican and other churches.

Once my son was at a trampolining competition at Armadale in WA. He was around 11 or 12.

He was outside playing; I was inside helping with running the competition.

A lady said come outside. Your son has had an accident. Outside in the car park, a group of people gathered around my son; he was leaning against a car. In front of him was a big puddle of water, and it was bright red. He was not wearing shoes and had stood on a broken bottle hidden in the pool of water (Aussie kids don't wear shoes much). A lady was holding a wad of tissues on the bottom of his foot, and big drops of blood dripped into the pool. My son was crying and obviously in pain.

The lady said, "I am a nurse; this is very serious. You have to take him straight to the hospital."

I felt the Holy Spirit wanted to show the group of people his presence, so I said, there's no need to take him to the hospital; Jesus is going to heal him now.

The lady said, "I don't care what you do; you will still have to take him to the hospital." So, with all the ladies looking on, I bent down, put my hand on his foot, and said, "In the name of Jesus, I command this foot to be healed, I command the bleeding to stop, I command the pain to stop." I said, "There we are. He is healed now."

The lady said, "We have to take him to the hospital. I said, "No, he is healed." (I thank her for her concern and compassion for my son), and she said, "Let's take him inside, and I will clean his foot, and we will have a look."

So, the mum followed us inside and lifted him onto the kitchen worktop.

She threw the wad of blood-soaked tissues in the bin, washed a cloth under the tap, and then wiped his foot. On the bottom of his foot was a red mark about 2 inches long, with no bleeding. He had stopped crying and was no longer in pain. I told my son you could go outside and play if you want, but put your shoes on this time.

The Holy Spirit did not instruct me to say anything to the group of ladies, and I went back to help in the competition. I don't know the lady's first name, but I believe she was Lenny Micro's mum in Armadale PCYC.

Once in a John Wimber Conference, John invited people who wanted prayers for healing to stand in the aisles. Then he said all those who felt led by the Holy Spirit to go and pray for them.

I felt led to pray for a lady sitting just a few chairs up from me who had gone to stand in the Aisles. I prayed for the lady, and immediately she fell onto the floor. (I was surprised this happened and did not catch her)

She lay on the floor for about half an hour. When she got up, she told me that she had been in a car crash some 5 or 6 years ago and had damaged her ribs and lungs so badly that only one lung functioned, even that one was defective. Since I prayed for her, their lungs had been completely healed, and that was the first time she had been able to take a deep full breath of air for 5 or 6 years.

At the same time, I also prayed for a lady with a damaged back; she also fell on the floor and lay there for some time; she was completely healed of her back problem when she got up.

I want to encourage you that even in a work environment, I have prayed for people to be healed and had them come back the following day and tell me they were healed. Please listen to the Holy Spirit, as sometimes he wants to do more than heal.

I was in a meeting held by the Word of Life Group in St Elizabeth's Church. We were having a cup of tea and some nibbles after the meeting. There was a lady with terrible weeping sores over her leg. I asked if I could pray for her, and she said yes, so with all the people gathered around (there was a nun there who was very interested in what I was about to do), I asked the Holy Spirit to come to guide me how I should pray.

To my surprise, I told this lady, "You have unforgiveness towards your daughter." She started to cry and said, "Yes, my daughter married against my wishes, and I have not spoken to her for 5 years."

I said, "This problem with your leg is caused by unforgiveness towards your daughter. Can I pray with you to forgive your daughter?" So, as she repented of having unforgiveness, the sores on her leg started to dry up and disappear until just red blotchy marks were left.

The lady later told me that the doctors were so concerned that if her leg did not get better soon, they might have had to amputate it to stop it from spreading to the rest of her body. I only met the lady once and did not remember her name.

I have given just a few brief examples of healing that you can do by listening to the Holy Spirit. I, again, acknowledge that I did nothing and have no power to heal; only the Power of God healed those people using the name of Jesus.

One day, I was praying, and the Holy Spirit said, "I want you to start an outreach center for drug addicts, alcoholics, and the homeless." So, I said, "Where will this be."

The Holy Spirit said, "Get in your car and drive to Bunbury and I will show you the place." So, I got in my car, drove to Bunbury, and parked in the city center.

The Holy Spirit said, "Walk down here, turn right, left, right," As I approached a building, he said, "This is the place."

I said, "Oh no, this cannot be the place. This is the Old Custom's House which houses the Australian Customs Dept." He said, "Go round the corner and read the notice on the door."

The notice on the door said the Australian Customs Dept has now moved to such and such a place. So, I contacted the Bunbury City Council, asked if I could have the building, and explained it was an outreach center for the homeless, drug addicts, and alcoholics. Bunbury City Council explained they were trying to sell the building to be developed as a cinema complex, but they liked the idea, and I could have the building until it was needed for the Cinema complex. So, I had the building for approximately—18 months to

2yrs. The Outreach Centre was established with help from my wife and friends John Helpers and David Mackenzie.

We also employed a lady full-time (Tone Panatela) as a counselor/assistant to help people run the center during the day.

The front room was a coffee shop with tables and chairs, a tv and video player, and a pool table. The middle rooms were a craft room, offices, and kitchen. At the back was a large hall, where we had set up keyboard drums, guitar, and amplifiers so teenagers could come in and jam, and also a table tennis table was set up.

All the facilities were provided at no cost to the people that came. Even tea, coffee, and soft drinks were provided for free. We also gave food to people who had problems and sometimes money if we felt they were genuine.

All the costs of the outreach center were borne by myself, John Helpers, and Dave Mackenzie. Our company Prima Personnel employed the lady administration assistant.

Directly across from the Old Custom's house is Yan get, a house where many of the inmates have mental health and associated problems, and they were also able to spend time in the outreach center. We offered the use of the Outreach Centre to the Brotherhood Fraternal, which was a group of Church Ministers; we felt led by the Holy Spirit that all the churches should unite and join in this ministry.

We offered them unconditionally that they could run whatever ministries they wanted without us interfering; we would be responsible for paying the bills. (I have covered their response in the section being persecuted). I previously spoke of my friends Malcolm and Gaik-Sim Holloway, who supported us in the venture. We invited Phil Howells from Newsday Church Perth; he came down with some church members and held a couple of meetings with 100 or 120 people packed into this small hall.

They were extraordinary meetings with the Holy Spirit moving in great power, with everyone being blessed. I thank Phil and his wife Jeanette for their support at this time.

The outreach center touched and blessed many people, and I will just share some of the many experiences.

One evening and Gaik were in the Outreach Centre, and a Baikie who came to the center came to speak to us. He was contemplating committing suicide (he was a drug addict). We prayed with him, and he gave his life to Jesus, and we prayed for him to be filled with the Holy Spirit. It turned out his father was a Baptist Minister.

After praying with him, we talked generally, and he said he would like a job and a girlfriend. So, we prayed with him to get a job and a girlfriend (this was on Sunday evening). On Wednesday or Thursday, he called in to see us and said he got a Job in Love's Buses as a mechanic on Monday, met a girl on Tuesday, and now had a girlfriend.

Several weeks later, he called to see us and said he was leaving Bunbury to go to Perth. I was surprised and asked why you wanted to leave when everything was well. He told me that God had told him to become a church minister, and he had enrolled in Bible College in Perth. So, he left, and I have forgotten his name, but I hope he is happy and well.

Another time some Chinese sailors came into the café area, and we started talking to them (Gaik-Sim could speak their language). We prayed with the 3 of them, and they gave their lives to Jesus, and we prayed for them to be filled with the Holy Spirit and a bible to return home with.

Over this period, we were very anointed by the Holy Spirit. I estimate that I was personally involved with over 300 people who were prayed for, received the gift of salvation, and were filled with the Holy Spirit.

Later Steve Smith and Murray Beecroft started holding meetings in the outreach center. They were also wonderful meetings where the power of God showed up.

Steve was led to move the church to the Railway Institute, and shortly after that, God closed the outreach center; the building was knocked down and turned into the cinema complex in Bunbury.

I just want to share a little about the Ministry of Elijah and how it is to turn the hearts of the fathers to the children and the children to the fathers.

One day at about 6:30 in the morning, I got a phone call from Steve Smith to say he could not take the morning service in the word of life center that morning. Could I take it for him? I asked the Holy Spirit what he wanted to do, and he gave me 5 scriptures.

The scriptures were about preparing yourself to enter into the presence of God.

So, when it came time for me to speak, I read the 5 scriptures and invited those who wanted to prepare themselves to come into God's presence to the front of the church. To my surprise, nearly everyone came forward. (Maybe 30 or so people)

I asked the Holy Spirit to come, and things got interesting; one guy started shouting out loud (evil spirits were delivering him) while others were weeping.

As the Holy Spirit instructed me to, I went up and ministered to individuals; sometimes, I had a word from the Lord for them, or I prayed for others. This weeping continued through the rest of the service, and after the service, people prayed for each other. When we returned for the evening service at 6:00 pm, some people were still weeping; God was doing a mighty work in some people's hearts.

Another example of the Spirit of Elijah is one Sunday in St. Nicholas Church, Australind, which was run by a nice guy called Glen Rebello. Glen asked if anyone had a word from the Lord that they could come to the front and speak.

I felt led by the Holy Spirit to go up the front and say, 2000 years ago, the people knew how much God loved them because Jesus was sent to display the father's love. They could hear Jesus, touch Jesus and experience the love that flowed from him. When Jesus ascended into heaven, he sent the Holy Spirit; it is the Holy Spirit's job to reveal God's love to us. Then I said, all those who want to experience God's love, come to the front, and I will pray and ask the Holy Spirit to come.

A good part of the church came to the front, and I prayed a very simple prayer, Holy Spirit, please come and reveal the father's love in the name of Jesus.

People started weeping at the front and others in their seats; this continued for a little while, and then Glen continued with the service. People wept through communion and the rest of the service.

After the service, people carried on weeping and ministered to each other. I went into a vestry room to pray on my own and thank God for what he had just done.

Glen and about 6 or 8 others came into the room, and Glen asked me to pray for him. The anointing was strong in that room; I remember Glen on his knees, with the whole group praying for him.

I left the room and shut the door; people in the main church were still weeping and ministering to each other, and no one seemed to want to leave. I asked the Holy Spirit if there was anything else he needed me to do, and he said no, so I went home.

I hope that the above has encouraged you that when the Holy Spirit instructs you to pray for him to come, he will.

When we are called to witness others and lead them to Jesus, it is just so simple if you listen to the Holy Spirit. Once my wife became friendly with the Sullivan Family in Bunbury, who had started going to church, they were a little unhappy with the church they had just started going to, so my wife suggested that they come to the Anglican Church we went to.

At the end of the service, as I was walking toward the family, the Holy Spirit said I want you to say to Ken, can I pray for you and your family to give your lives to Jesus. I thought this family hardly knew me. This was not a good idea, but

I was obedient, and as I was introduced to Ken, Catherine, and his family, I said, " Can I pray for you and your family to give your lives to Jesus and be filled with the Holy Spirit.

To my surprise, they all said yes, so I prayed for mum, dad, and the other teenagers, and the Holy Spirit touched them and ministered to them.

Similarly, my friend John Helpers knew me before I became a Christian, and while he was working overseas, I came to know Jesus. He came to work at Millennium Chemicals (SCM), where a group of Christians met during our lunch break.

I invited John to come along, and the Holy Spirit said do not mention my name in talking to John. So, as we talked to John about his experiences overseas and where he had been working, the Holy Spirit started to anoint me, and I started to shake. I became very embarrassed, and John stared at me; this shaking lasted for about twenty minutes.

Then the Holy Spirit said to me, "Now ask him if you can pray with him to give his life to Jesus and be filled with the Holy Spirit just as you have been."

I thought this was crazy; he had received no gospel message, and no one had been talking about anything with Jesus all lunchtime, but I was obedient. I told John exactly what the Holy Spirit asked me to say; John was a little taken aback, and so were all the others, but then he said yes, I would love that. So, we gathered around John, and we prayed with him as he gave his life to Jesus, and we prayed for him to be filled with the Holy Spirit, and he spoke in tongues.

Just a final witness about praying for people for salvation…

Dawn and Mike Anderson had friends who called to see them weekly before a rotary club meeting.

They told me they had tried to talk to him about Jesus many times, but it was like a brick wall. They asked me to come and talk to the guy. (I don't know his name)

His father was a Baptist minister and did not believe in the gifts of the Holy Spirit or speaking in tongues. I said, "I will not argue with you, let's stand, and I will ask the Holy Spirit to come, and you can experience it yourself." He said okay, so we stood, and I prayed for the Holy Spirit to come.

This guy was immaculately dressed to go to his meeting, and the Holy Spirit came on him with great heat. He started sweating profusely, but abnormally so; sweat was running down his face and dripping from his nose, his hair became soaking wet, his shirt became wet and see-through, and he turned into a mess, so much so that Dawn went and got him a towel and this was in winter.

Eventually, I said are you ready for us to Pray for you to give your life to Jesus and he said yes; he repented of his sins and asked Jesus, into his life, I asked whether you wanted me to pray for you to be filled with the Holy Spirit, he said yes, so we prayed for him to be filled with the Holy Spirit. Then I asked, "Do you want to receive the gift of speaking in tongues?" He said yes, so we prayed for him to speak in tongues, and he did.

I know God mightly touched that man and transformed his life that night. In the natural, we could have argued with that man for months, but when the Holy Spirit turns up, all arguments cease.

I encourage you not to be afraid to minister to people of other religions. Once, a security guard was at the gate at Millennium Chemicals; he was a Buddhist. I started talking to him about Jesus and felt led to give him a Christian book to read. He said he would read it as long as I read one of his books on Buddhism. The Holy Spirit said yes, take it and read it.

So, I took his book on Buddhism home and started reading it; in the middle of the book was a section on seeking enlightenment, and there was a warning in this section about seeking enlightenment. It warned of a story about a young

Buddhist monk seeking enlightenment when Jesus appeared to him and said I am the way, the truth, and the life; there is no other way to God except through me. When the young monk reported to his teacher what had happened, the teacher said he had gone mad, and they locked him in solitary confinement without food or water until he came to his right mind.

I went back to the security guard and pointed out that they were seeking enlightenment, and when they found it, they denied the truth that Jesus was their savior. He left that job shortly after, and I saw him in a petrol station some 6 months later. He came over and said that now he and his family were Christians and went to church every Sunday because I listened to the Holy Spirit and read a book.

And again, I felt led to start talking to a Muslim named Tony at Worsley Alumina. He asked if I would go to the mosque with him, and the Holy Spirit said yes.

I said yes, I would go to the mosque with you.

He was surprised and said every other Christian he had asked said no. I felt the Holy Spirit say to me, go to the library, get a copy of the Koran, and read it. So, I asked if they had a copy of the Koran. One assistant said yes, but the only copy we have is in the reference library, and you can't borrow it; the other librarian was listening and said no one has ever asked for the Koran, so let him take it home.

So, I took it home and read it under the direction of the Holy Spirit. He showed me which pages he wanted me to photocopy. So, I went to Tony and said, " Look, I want to show you some things in your Koran. I showed him how Christians, Jews, and Muslims are all worshipping the same God; I showed him where the Koran says that Mary is to be revered and where it says that Jesus is the Messiah.

He said that his brother was a teacher of the Koran (Imam?), and he would ask his opinion. He came back a week or two later and said that his brother agreed with what I said; he also told me that his wife was a catholic and had always wanted to go to church with her but felt it was a problem because he was a Muslim.

So now, he didn't see any problem and started attending the Catholic Church with his wife. The Holy Spirit knows the key needed to unlock people's minds so they can have a relationship with Jesus. We must listen to the Holy Spirit and let him use the key through us.

I write this next section to encourage those Christians who have been praying for someone to be converted for a long time.

I was visiting someone in Bunbury Prison once, and when I came out into the car park, I had my bible in my hand; a man noticed it and made some comment which opened up a conversation.

I spoke to this guy who wasn't a Christian for nearly an hour, witnessing what God had done in my life. At the end of the conversation, I invited him to the Vineyard Church in Australind, where I was going that evening.

He came along to the church and sat next to a lady near the front. Pastor Don O'Shaughnessy appealed to anyone who wanted to get right with God to go to the front at the end of the service. This guy got up and went to the front. They prayed with him, he gave his life to Jesus, and they prayed for him to be filled with the Holy Spirit.

He was weeping, and the lady who sat next to him. After the service, he approached me and thanked me for speaking to him and inviting him. The lady with him was a friend who told me she had been praying for him to know Jesus for 9 years. I am sorry, I don't know the lady's or the man's names, only they were from Bridgetown.

I encourage you that no matter what the outward signs appear, believe that God will answer your prayer no matter how long the answer takes to come.

Sometimes, God does not do what you expect but just be open to the Holy Spirit. I was once led to start meetings in Hudson Road Centre in

Bunbury; on a Sunday afternoon (I thought I was starting a church), 2 ladies came. (Jenny and Cammy)

I was puzzled at the low turnout as I expected many people. At the back of the center was a playground which could only be reached through the hall we were in. Three aboriginal children came and asked if they could use the playground; I said yes, on one condition, we pray for you first, so we prayed for the aboriginal children.

The Holy Spirit came on them; they stayed with us and didn't go to the playground. Next week there were more; we read to them from the bible, sang songs, and prayed with them. The Holy Spirit came on some of them very powerfully. After only a couple of weeks, over 30 aboriginal children varied in age from 6 to 19. They all gave their lives to Jesus except the very oldest girl, they were all prayed for to be filled with the Holy Spirit, and everyone was prayed for each week. I then had to stop this work because my son was in the State Trampolining Team, and I had to drive up to Perth 2-to 3 weeks out of 4.

I know the Holy Spirit accomplished what he wanted in that area. The most moving experience for me was after we prayed for an aboriginal boy about 12 years of age. He looked at me with tears and said, "I know my mum doesn't love me, but now I know Jesus does." I was not expecting all these aboriginal kids to be open to the Holy Spirit and go with the flow; he may be doing something different from what you think.

This next section is on ministry to other churches and denominations. Once I was sent to the Seventh Day Adventist Church, Bunbury, by the Holy Spirit, it started with him sending me to a Revelation Seminar. I was sent to the Pastor with a message for him from the Holy Spirit. The word I had for the Pastor was that God would make the latter end of his ministry great if he obeyed the Holy Spirit, and there would be a great harvest.

I attended his church every Saturday and also other meetings during the week. I tried to explain that none of the Seventh-Day Adventist teachings were beneficial to him. He was saved by belief in the name of Jesus, and none of the works he did or his church doctrine were worth anything. I asked if I could pray with him to be filled with the Holy Spirit, but he was not keen.

To cut the story short, after 8 or 9 months, the Holy Spirit told me to tell him that on a certain date (it was about 6 weeks away), I would stand in his church and pray for people to be filled with the Holy Spirit.

Therefore, let me give a little testimony each week so the Holy Spirit can prepare the people's hearts.

He had a meeting with his elders and got back to me and said, "We will not allow you to give personal testimonies, nor will we allow you to stand in our church and pray for people."

Anyway, the date came, and that morning I took the dog for a walk, and the Holy Spirit fell on me and gave me this long teaching about why they were saved because of what Jesus had done, not because they were Seventh Day Adventists. So, I went to the service and noticed something very unusual, all the men wore the same clothes, it was a uniform, dark black/grey trousers, a blazer shirt, and a tie, but a guy was sitting in shorts, a t-shirt with no sleeves, and thongs.

When he wanted me to stand and speak, I asked the Holy Spirit, and he said to wait and see what would happen. As the service progressed, this guy was introduced as the guest speaker; he ran one of their youth camps at Boddington. I think they expected him to talk about his youth ministry. Instead, he got up and said what the Holy Spirit had said to me that morning. He challenged them that they were saved because they believed in Jesus for no other reason.

When he finished speaking, the Holy Spirit said to me, get and go up on the platform, so I walked up on the stage and took hold of the microphone stand. Immediately two people came to either side of me and tried to push me off the stage, but I was stronger than they were and refused to budge; they became very embarrassed and stopped pushing me and stood on either side.

I testified how I was filled with the Holy Spirit and invited anyone who wanted to be filled with the Holy Spirit to stand. No one stood; I asked the Holy Spirit what he wanted me to do, and he said to be patient and stand and wait. So, after a little time (which seemed like hours up there on my own).

One guy asked, "Is it you're teaching that you must speak in tongues to be filled with the Holy Spirit?". I said, "I have no teachings; God sent me here to pray for you, but just for your information, speaking in tongues is a gift of the Holy Spirit; you can be filled with the Holy Spirit and not speak in tongues."

Another guy asked a question, and I said I am not here to hold a discussion or debate; I am here to pray for people to be filled with the Holy Spirit. Those who want to be prayed for to be filled with the Holy Spirit had better stand now. Twelve people stood out of the crowd of 100. So,

I prayed from the stage for those people to be filled with the Holy Spirit, then I sat down.

After the meeting, some people who had stood (mainly teenagers) came up to me and said it was the most amazing experience they had ever had.

I said to myself well, now we are beginning to get somewhere, but the Holy Spirit said, "You have accomplished what you came for; I don't want you to come to this church anymore," and so I said goodbye to all the people I had met there and never went there again.

I was also sent to the Jehovah's Witnesses and had many related incidents, but I will include this one item.

There was a lady in a wheelchair, and after one of the Jehovah's Witnesses meetings, I went up to her, started speaking to her, and asked if I could pray for her to get out of the wheelchair. She said yes, but the lady with her said she had to take her back to the older adults' home, and there was no time to pray for her. So, I arranged with the older lady to go home and pray with her there on Thursday.

When I got to the home on Thursday, one of the Jehovah's Witness Elders was sitting with her; he said sorry, we could not allow you to pray with this lady. I said it's nothing to do with you she invited me. So, I asked the lady if I could pray with her, and she said no, so I asked her why not. She said I thought you were one of the brothers (Jehovah's Witness).

I said, "I am a Jehovah's Witness, and I have been coming to your church for over 6 months." The elder said, "You are not a Jehovah's Witness, and you are not one of us because our teaching is we do not believe in healings and miracles today because they died out with the apostles." So, I said, "Why am I not Jehovah's Witness?" He said, "You have to do a bible study course with the elders, and then you have to be baptized as a Jehovah's Witness."

I said, "No problem, I can do all that." His eyes lit up, and he said, "So you are interested in becoming a Jehovah's Witness?" I said, "Yes, I can attend the bible study, be baptized as a Jehovah's Witness, and then can I pray for this lady to be healed and get out of this wheelchair."

"No," he said. "We don't believe in healings and miracles." I walked away shaking my head in disbelief; why would you condemn someone to the rest of their life in a wheelchair to prove some point of the doctrine of your church.

I never got to pray for that lady to be healed.

My final testimony on being sent to other churches…

Once my son was in a trampolining competition in Armadale; he wasn't competing until around noon. I felt the Holy Spirit say I want you to go to church, so I got in my car and drove; he directed me where to go, right, left, etc..; this is it. (Alliance Church)

So, I went in a little early, so I sat and prayed; then, a guy came and spoke to me for a little while. He was very nice. The service started, and the praise team ran through some songs, and then came an awkward silence; I said to the guy I spoke to that I had a word from the Lord and could I speak it out. He went and asked the Pastor and came back and said Yes.

I spoke out the word, which was very simple, God loved them very much; he was pleased with their progress and wanted to bless them. When I finished, someone else started prophesying, then someone else, and so on for nearly 30 minutes.

I had to leave to get back for my son's competition, so I sneaked out and walked across the car park; when the Pastor came out and shouted Stop after me, I turned around and thought, now I'm in trouble. He said, thank you very much; I said what for? He said you don't understand, none of my people have ever given a prophecy before, and I can't believe they did it.

I want to share that God is interested in even the small insignificant area of your life, I attended a prayer counseling school in Perth some time ago (VMTC).

On the last day, the Holy Spirit said to donate $50 to the work of VMTC. I said, Lord, I only have $60, and I kept it to buy a present for my son and daughter. He said to put in the $50, so I put in the $50 and had $10 left. Then to buy a present for my son and daughter, the Holy Spirit told me to go to a certain shop in Bunbury.

When I went into the shop, I wondered what I should buy; he said to go to the left-hand back of the shop; when I got there, I saw a row of T-shirts reduced to $5 each.

I thought I didn't know the correct size to buy for my kids. The Holy Spirit indicated to me which 2 T-shirts to buy. (They had Jurassic Park Dinosaur motives)

I took them home and gave them to my kids; they fit perfectly. My son was so pleased that he did not take it off for a week. (I even slept in it)

I just want to make you aware that God is interested in the minutest detail if you are willing to obey him.

I just want to say that if you have kids or teenagers, do not limit what God will do with them.

When my son Alec was about 7, his teacher told him that his friend Ryan had chicken pox and would not be coming to school for a while. My son told the teacher that he wanted to play with his friend the next day and would pray and ask Jesus to heal the chicken pox.

His mum brought Ryan to school the next day as the chicken pox had suddenly disappeared, and he wanted to come to school. My son stood up in Church that Sunday without anyone asking him, and he gave a personal testimony of how Jesus had healed his friend so he could play with him.

Once a lady came to our home group with her daughter, about 12 (the same age as my daughter Jenna). The daughter had very bad asthma. A couple of days later, there was a school sports day, and the girl wanted to run in the school sports. (But could not because of her asthma)

My daughter prayed for her and envisioned her crossing the finishing line first. Asthma left her, and she ran in the school sports a few days later, crossed the finishing line first, and won her race.

In ministry to children, be careful not to interfere with what the Holy Spirit is doing.

Once my son Alec had his friend David Bill come for a sleepover. I asked his parents, and they said it was okay to take him to church.

So, we went to the Australind Vineyard Church. Alec and David stood on the chairs when everyone stood for worship. But then they started falling off the chairs, climbing back up and falling off again, laughing and giggling. I was going to lean over and tell them to stop.

The Holy Spirit said do not stop what they are doing. The people around started at us with obvious annoyance as these kids were quite noisy as they fell off the chairs and got back up while laughing and giggling. (They were about 12 years old)

As we drove home in the car, I asked David what he thought of the church. (I knew he had never been before). His reply surprised me; he said, "I believe in God now."

I said, "Why?" He said, "Because God played with Alec and me and kept pushing us off the chair."

Please ask the Holy Spirit before you rush in and stop a work of the Holy Spirit.

When I was 13, I went to confirmation class with my friends in an Anglican church in Swansea. We started laughing at one of these classes where the Priest was talking about the Holy Spirit.

No one had said anything funny; the more the Priest told us to stop, the more we laughed. He got very angry. It was not until I went to a John Wimber conference in 1994 that as this Priest had talked to us about the Holy Spirit, the Holy Spirit had fallen on us and released the Spirit of Joy. The Priest did not understand because he had no relationship with the Holy Spirit. But for many years, I knew something strange and wonderful had happened that night but was not sure what it was.

I want to share using the gift of prophecy (or word of knowledge). One evening I got a phone call from Steve Smith, Pastor of the word of life center, it was 6:30, and he asked if I could take a bible study course at 7:00 pm because he was unwell. So, I set off for this meeting, and as I went, I asked the Holy Spirit what he wanted to do; he said he wanted to teach on prophecy.

There were about 30 people there, so I started explaining how to use the gift of prophecy. I explained that it was exercised by faith and that if you believed that the Holy Spirit had spoken to you, all you had to do was repeat it to the person for whom it was intended.

I prayed and invited the Holy Spirit to come and said to the people that a Spirit of Prophecy will sweep through the room and touch some of you. A girl was 12 years old; the Holy Spirit said to call her to the front. So, I invited her up to the front.

I said, "God will tell you something for someone here; all you have to do is repeat it." She immediately pointed at a lady in the second row and said, "God says you are a drug addict, you are in rebellion to me, you only come here to look respectable, and you don't believe in me."

The lady burst into tears and said it was all true. The people gathered around her and prayed with her; she repented, gave her life to Jesus, and prayed to be filled with the Holy Spirit. Then I invited her up to the front and invited her to give a prophecy to someone else.

And so, the Holy Spirit gave her some words to speak to another man, and then I called him up to the front. The meeting lasted 2-3 hours, with many people being ministered and praying for and learning to use the gift of prophecy.

CHAPTER 9

THE PERSECUTION

IF YOU HEAR FROM God, if the Holy Spirit gives you instructions and you obey them, you will be persecuted if God has chosen you for a specific task in his kingdom work. (This persecution will come from the church, not the world)

Before I share these things, I want to explain that this is written from my wife's and my point of view. The other people involved may have their version of how the events unfolded. For certain, God knows the truth, and he is the judge.

I shared earlier how a guy came and spoke to my wife and me, how we became Christians, how I read the bible for 4 to 6 hours—every night, and how God spoke to me.

And so, the guy who spoke to us invited us to his church which was not a mainline Pentecostal Church. (As soon as we were their problems started), within 2 weeks of being a Christian, they would say to us; you need to be baptized.

I asked God; he said no. So, I would say no; then they would say, why not? I would say because God says no.

They would say you have only been a Christian for 2 weeks; how can you hear God's voice. I don't care if God says no and I am not being baptized.

They would say that you are going straight to hell if you go out this door and get knocked down and killed. (They said this because they had two teachings which God speaking to me said were wrong, (1) Anyone who was not baptized or speaking in tongues was going to hell, (2) Because they are co-inheritors with Christ, then they must be equal to Jesus.)

The Church leadership became increasingly frustrated as time passed because we would not obey them (we listened to God) and questioned their teachings (as God instructed us to).

On Sunday, the Pastor gave a sermon where he mocked Jimmy Swagger by putting on an American accent and saying stupid things. I looked at my wife; she looked at me; something was seriously wrong with this church. After about 6 weeks of being a Christian, the Pastor got fed up with us and came around our house with his chief elder.

They wanted us to submit to the church authority and be baptized in their church. My wife (under the inspiration of the Holy Spirit) said that John says to test every spirit that will not confess Christ is not from God. Then she said to the Pastor, "I want to hear you say that Jesus is your Lord and Savior." He became very angry, said, "You are hypocrites, banned from coming to my church again," and stormed out.

The elder was very embarrassed, apologized for his Pastor's outburst, and left. So, after being Christians for 6 weeks, we were banned from a church purely because we listened to God and obeyed what he instructed us to do.

I have never had the opportunity to thank the guy who came and spoke to us in the car park and came to our house; I thank him for the blessing he gave my family and me.

So, for a year, we did not go to church, and then for the benefit of my Father and Mother-in-law, we joined an Anglican church in Bunbury; under the first Priest, everything was normal; we had our problems as everyone else. The first Priest left, and a new priest came.

To be sensitive and not defamatory, I have deliberately left the details vague while conveying the overall effect.

The new Priest came, and most of the time, things were fine. We did not agree that my wife and I were split up, so we ministered in separate ministry teams. Even that was not so bad. Then he got married; I was looking forward to his wife coming as she had been in charge of a ministry team herself, and I was hoping to learn from her. She did not involve herself with the ministry team and seemed cold and aloof.

About this time, I started being given the scripture John 9:22 "For the Jews had decided that anyone who acknowledged that Jesus was the Christ would be put out of the synagogue."

I started to feel I would be thrown out of the church. One day, as I was in a meeting with the Bishop of Bunbury. I felt the Holy Spirit come on me, and I heard the Holy Spirit say to me beware the Ides of March, and then I heard myself say to the Bishop of Bunbury, on March the 17th, someone will come and speak to you, and you will permit them for me to be thrown out of the church.

And so, things continued for approximately one year.

All the time, I was puzzled as to why this Priest's wife was so cold and aloof, and so one morning at approx. 6:00 am (it was light), I was praying and asking the Holy Spirit why was this lady so aloof, and I was suddenly taken in the spirit and stood outside a house; it was very dark and late at night (I guess midnight and the house appeared to be located in withers estate), as I stood outside the house and looked at the wall of the house, the wall disappeared, and I could see into the bedroom. This poor lady was being raped, begging the man to stop, but he would not.

One week, things came to a head when my wife was working on a school fete on Sunday, so rather than go to the Anglican Church, I went up the road to a Baptist church. When I got there, the Holy Spirit told me to give a message to the church.

I asked the Pastor if I could speak it out; he said I could not but tell him what the message was first.

I told the Pastor that God said he did not want the church to split. I again asked if I could speak the message out, but he said no, so I sat down. (Shortly afterward, the church did split into two)

When we went to the Anglican church healing team meeting that week, the Priest's wife was there for the first time since she had come to the church. She verbally attacked my wife and me, saying they had a lousy meeting the previous Sunday and it was our fault because we weren't there.

We were a bit taken aback; I cannot remember if my visit to the Baptist Church was brought up, but I suspect it was.

Anyway, my wife and I discussed the events when we got home and arranged a meeting with the Priest and his wife the following day. We said they had lost confidence in us and our ministry, and we felt it was best if we laid down our ministries and didn't do anything in that church for a while.

On Saturday, I went to a Word of Life (a sort of bible study) meeting held by John and Margaret. John went to the Anglican Church and his wife Margaret to the Catholic; the meeting was Margaret's and had nothing to do with the Anglican Church.

At the meeting came an Anglican couple who brought a young man named Bradley who had just converted to the Lord. They started witnessing how they had brought Bradley to the Lord and other things. Now there was nothing wrong with what they were saying except it was Margaret's meeting, and, in their enthusiasm, they took it over. Then they said let's pray for John (who had previously had a stroke), so I asked the Holy Spirit, and he said no, so I said to them, the Holy Spirit is not instructing me to pray for John. Then they said, well, we'd pray, and you can pray with us, so I said ok.

So, they prayed for John with me assisting, and as the praying went along, I got dragged further into it until I was fully praying with the others. (I could see Margaret was getting annoyed).

Anyway, the meeting closed and I went home not thinking too much about it, except I knew I had disobeyed the Holy Spirit's instruction. (This was a Saturday evening)

On Sunday, we felt led not to take the kids to church but went to the Anglican Church as normal; as we were about to go inside, the Holy Spirit very clearly said to me, "Whatever you do today, do not stand and speak."

And so, we went inside and sat down; instead of starting as normal, the Priest went up to the pulpit/book rest and started to speak. (Note I do not remember the exact words, but this is very approximately)

"My wife and I spent 3 hours last night counseling someone after Michael prayed for them. We believe his Ministry and his wife's Ministry are false and not from God, and we believe they are deluded, and we do not believe any of his prophecies are from God. If he wants to stay in this church, he must repent and renounce all the prophecies he has given as not being from God."

I stupidly stood up to speak and was immediately grabbed hold of by 3 or 4 people, walked to the church door, and expelled. (Understand this was not done roughly, Anglicans are such gentle people).

As I went out the door, I shouted out this church belongs to Jesus, not you. But there was the voice of the Holy Spirit "Didn't I tell you not to stand and speak, you dummy."

I went to John and Margaret's house that afternoon to apologize. Only John was in (Margaret was out), and I asked John for forgiveness for him having to go through three hours of counseling. He said he did not know what the Priest was talking about. All that had happened was that Margaret was annoyed that the Word of Life had been taken over by the Anglican couple and had rung the Priest to complain.

I rang Margaret later to apologize; she said she didn't have a problem with me; she was angry with the Anglican couple who took over her meeting and rang the Priest to complain about them. When she mentioned my name, the Priest became very angry, so he frightened her, and she cut short the conversation. So, I asked how long she was on the phone, and she said around 5 minutes.

I asked her if she would ring the Priest and explain she did not have a problem with me that day, but she said she did not want to get involved.

And so, to cut the story short, we tried to meet with the Priest and his wife to discuss the issues, but they would not.

I met with the Bishop; I reminded him that I predicted I would be thrown out of the church a year earlier. He was annoyed and said I engineered the whole thing to bring the prophecy to pass. We asked him to arrange a meeting with the Priest and his wife, but they refused.

There are continuations in the story regarding the Anglican issues, but they are minor.

The rest of this story is played out in the wider Christian community, particularly the church leaders, where the Priest meets with other church leaders.

As I said, the Holy Spirit told me shortly after this event to start an outreach center. He also told us that we were not to minister from there but first to offer it to the churches. So, on 3 occasions, we wrote letters and offered the outreach center to the Brother's Fraternal. I also had a meeting with 2 of them (and my 2 friends previously mentioned). They declined the free use of the outreach center and wrote a letter to all churches in Bunbury saying that my ministry was not from God and that I was unwilling to submit to any authority.

I found that strange as we were willing to hand the outreach center over to them, they could run it as they wanted jointly with other churches, and we would be responsible only for paying the bills. And again, we asked to come under the umbrella of the vineyard church in Perth, but they said no.

In 1995, I went to a vineyard conference in Perth; as I drove up from Bunbury to Perth, I thought, at least I can get away from the persecution now.

The Holy Spirit said you would be persecuted in Perth, but you will receive a great blessing there.

So, on the first morning of the conference, they asked for volunteers to be on the ministry team to meet at lunchtime. So, I went to the meeting, and to my surprise, a lady asked me to sit on my own while she spoke to the rest of the people. They were invited onto the ministry team and given a little dot on their badges. Then she came over, and a pastor from Bunbury appeared, and he sat with me; they told me that the Pastor of the Perth vineyard church had decided not to let me minister in his church. So, I said, ok, if that's what he wants.

So, I arranged a meeting with the Pastor of the Perth vineyard church and asked him why he had requested I not minister in his church at this

John Wimber Conference. He said he had heard everything about me from the pastors in Bunbury.

I said, but what does the Holy Spirit say. He said all the pastors in Bunbury are godly men, and they have a problem with you. Why are you not willing to pray and ask God but rather listen to men. He repeated that these were godly men, listening to their advice, and he would not let me, minister. We also discussed other things which are of no consequence.

The Holy Spirit said to me the following day, now go and get your blessing. I said what do you mean. He said to go up to John Wimber and ask him to bless you. John was in a wheelchair, so I introduced myself to him. I said John, please will you pray for me to receive a double portion of the anointing on your life. He laughed and said sit down and let's have a chat, so we spoke for about 20 minutes (all this time, the anointing had come on me, and I was shaking violently). Then he said, the Holy Spirit has instructed me to grant your request, and he leaned overlaid his hands on me and prayed for me. It was like an electric current was passing through me.

I thanked John and moved away as there was a queue of people. I have been to 3 John Wimber conferences and have never seen him touch or lay hands on anyone before, so I know I have been blessed with something very special.

Regarding the persecution I received in Bunbury, I hold no anger or resentment toward the people involved. I know, in part, it was my fault for disobeying the Holy Spirit on two occasions. Some of the Pastors later understood that what was being said about me was incorrect.

I thank Don O'Shaughnessy of the Australind vineyard church and Stuart Devenish, the chairman of the brothers fraternal. I have tried not to judge anyone, just the facts so that you understand you will be persecuted if you listen to God and do whatever he says.

I can give more examples of being persecuted, but I believe this is sufficient, so you understand that you will be persecuted if you listen to God and obey his instructions.

CHAPTER 10

The Desert Experience—Being Tested

CHRISTIANS TODAY DO NOT seem to be taught that one of the reasons they are here is so that God can test them.

It says in Genesis that God tested Abraham and said to him, take your only son and go to the region of Moriah and sacrifice him there. When God gave the commandments to moss, he invited the people to come closer, but the people said to the moss that he should speak to them, but do not have God speak to us or we will die. Moses replied, do not be afraid God has come to test you so that the fear of God will be with you to keep you from sinning.

And again, through Moses, God says, if you follow my decrees and are careful to obey all my commands, I will send rain in its season, and the ground will yield its crop and the trees of the field their fruit to you. (i.e., if you obey God, he will bless you)

But if you will not listen to me and carry out all these commands, and if you reject my decrees and abhor my laws, then I will do this to you, I will bring upon your sudden terror, wasting diseases and fever, that will destroy your sight and drain away from your life. (i.e., if you disobey God, he will curse you)

This is a form of testing. In the New Testament, things have not changed regarding testing.

Jesus told Peter, Simon, and Simon that Satan has asked to sift you like wheat, but I have prayed that your strength may not fail.

Jesus was himself tested by being obedient even unto death.

When Ananias fell dead after lying to Peter about how much they sold some property for, Sapphira came in, and Peter tested her with the same question he asked Ananias; she also gave the wrong answer and fell dead. (They were being tested)

In James, it says, consider it pure joy, my brothers, whenever you face trials of many kinds because you know that the testing of your faith develops perseverance.

And again, blessed is the man who perseveres under trial because he will receive the crown of life when he has stood the test.

In Revelation to the Church in Smyrna, Jesus says, I tell you the devil will put some of you in prison to test you, and you will suffer persecution for 10 days.

I write these things above to encourage you that you will be tested and that being persecuted is part of the test. How you react to the people persecuting you is part of the test. The test is also in overcoming habits or sins in our lives that are obstacles to us drawing closer to God and moving up the levels in our spiritual journey.

I want to share how God tests you and how he deals with you differently depending on your spiritual journey.

Before becoming a Christian, I had an addiction to watching TV and pornography. When I became a Christian, I knew this was wrong and tried not to do these things. It wasn't easy to overcome as it started at a very early age of about 8 when I would read my father's magazines. When I went to one of the John Wimber conferences, one of the speakers gave a talk on the subject and invited people to stand who wanted to be set free from pornography.

I stood and was touched very powerfully by God and set free from this problem. A lady came up to me afterward and offered to pray for me. Eventually, I agreed, and she had a word from God for me; the word was "Switch off the TV."

This simple statement was to have a profound effect on my life later.

God did deliver me from this problem, and for years I never watched tv or anything pornographic. (at least 6 or 7 years)

One day during a church service, the Holy Spirit told me that I had been a little child growing up in the Lord, and now it was time for me to become an adult.

He said he had been protecting me from all the faults in my character (including watching tv and pornography), and now I had to overcome these things with my strength. I argued with the Holy Spirit, saying what he was saying was not by scripture, but it was no use; I knew that the anointing I used to have had been lifted.

And so began the long, painful journey, where I slipped back into the old habit of watching TV programs and accessing internet pornography. I had lots of arguments with God where I complained I would much prefer to be a little child under his protection rather than having to fight this problem in my strength. (It even worried that I might actually like this sin more than I loved God.)

And so, this went on for some years (maybe 6 years) with some warnings given to me by my wife (under the guidance of the Holy Spirit).

The Lord was slowly coming to the point where he said, " This is no longer accepted; you must stop this habit.

And so, I had a minor incident in my Jeep, which was so strange that I reversed into a wall. (Completely unexplainable, I expected to go forward but instead reversed into a wall)

I understood this was a warning from God and stopped watching the TV, but over time forgot the warning and slipped back into watching TV.

My next warning was pretty severe (if it were not so serious, it would be funny). I had a similar unexplainable accident where I drove my Rolls Royce through a garage wall and into the Garden (Completely demolishing the wall).

I was half in and half out of the car at the time, and I do not understand how I was not crushed between the wall and the car. After the accident, I prayed about what was going on, and the Holy Spirit said my time of grace had ended, and I was to stop watching TV and pornography. He also said if I did not obey the instruction to stop watching TV and pornography, my next car crash would be catastrophic.

Then he said something surprising: "Your father had the same problem, and I gave him the same three warnings in car crashes."

When I thought back, my father also had 3 strange car crashes, 1) he reversed into 2 cars simultaneously in a car park. 2) He dropped a cigarette lighter and drove into a lamppost when he bent down to pick it up; 3) He turned his car upside down at 70 mph when a truck pulled out in front of him and slid down the road on the roof of his car in peak rush hour on a motorway.

After I had finished praying, my wife came in, who had also been praying in another room, and said God would bring a real catastrophic car crash that would affect the whole family if I did not stop what I was doing. The latest events are recent, and I am trying to overcome these problems with God's help.

I am sharing these events with you because we are being tested, and some of the problems we have in our lives are sent or allowed by God because we are in rebellion against him. If we are having ongoing problems, we need to pray and ask God what the root cause of the problem is and how he wants us to deal with it.

There is no rule or regulation; it is how the Holy Spirit leads us; what may be acceptable for one person may not be acceptable for another because of where they are on their spiritual journey.

Read the letters to the churches in Revelation if you want a real understanding of how and why God tests us.

I want to add that you will never emerge with real power and authority in your Ministry for God unless you have gone through a desert experience and have been tested like Jesus was tested by satan. satan will always have a hold over you.

CHAPTER 11

The Blessing

If you obey the Holy Spirit, you will be blessed. If you continually disobey the Holy Spirit, you will be corrected.

The blessing you receive is spiritual, but as the spiritual and the physical world are very closely linked, you will also experience blessing in health, wealth, relationships, etc.

This is the same as for people from the bible in the past, Abraham, Isaac, Jacob, Joseph, David, and Solomon. As well as receiving spiritual blessings, they also received great wealth and power.

Do not be distressed when you are persecuted; believe that you will be blessed as you submit to the Holy Spirit and obey him.

In the persecution I received from almost all the church leaders in Bunbury, he gave me this scripture: I will make those of the Synagogue of satan come and bow down before you. And again, he said, I had prepared a table before you in the presence of your enemies,

I anoint your head with oil, and your cup rennet over.

We obtain the blessing by one very simple thing: pleasing God in everything we do. Jesus was a man attested by God because he pleased God.

God said, "This is my beloved son I am well pleased with." Jesus was obedient to the instructions given to him by the Holy Spirit, and even though this resulted in persecution to his death, he received great blessings because of his obedience. Because of Jesus' obedience, that blessing flowed onto the whole of creation.

In revelations, Jesus gives some amazing promises if we persevere and obey the Holy Spirit in all circumstances.

To him who overcomes, I will give the right to eat of the tree of life, which is in the paradise of God. He who overcomes will not be hurt at all by the second death.

To him who overcomes, I will give some of the hidden manna; I will also give him a white stone with a new name written on it known only to him who receives it.

I will give authority over the nations to him who overcomes and does my will to the end. He will rule over them with an iron scepter and dash them to pieces like pottery. Just as I have received authority from my Father, I will also give him the morning star.

He who overcomes will be dressed in white; I will never blot out his name from the book of life but acknowledge his name before my Father and his angels.

God that overcomes, I will make a pillar in the temple of my God, and never again will he leave it. I will write on him the name of my God and the name of the city of my God, the new Jerusalem, which is coming down out of heaven from my God; and I will also write on him my new name.

To him who overcomes, I will give the right to sit with me on my throne just as I overcame and sat down with my Father on his throne.

I would like to remember some of the blessings people in the bible received when they obeyed God.

Then God blessed Noah and his sons, saying to them. "Be fruitful and increase in number and fill the earth. The fear and dread of you will fall on the earth's beasts, the birds of the air, upon every creature that moves along the ground, and upon all the sea's fish; they are given into your hands. Everything that moves will be food for you. I now give you everything just as I gave you the green plants."

After Lot had departed from him, the Lord said to Abram, "Lift your eyes and look north, south, east, and west. I will give all the land you see to you and your offspring forever. I will make your offspring like the dust of the earth so that if Anyone could count the dust, then your offspring could be counted. Go walk through the length and breadth of the land, for I am giving it to you."

Again, the Lord said to Abram, "Do not be afraid; I am your shield, your very great reward." Moreover, finally, the Lord said to Abraham, "Because you have done this and not withheld your only son, I will surely bless you and make your descendants as numerous as the sky and sand on the sea shore. Your descendants will take possession of the cities of their enemies, and through your offspring, all nations on earth will be blessed because you have obeyed me."

At Marah, the Lord made a law and a decree for the Israelites, and there he tested them. He said, "If you listen carefully to the voice of the Lord your God and do what is right in his eyes. If you pay attention to his commands and keep all his decrees, I will not bring any diseases I brought on the Egyptians, for I am the Lord who heals you."

At Mount Sinai, the Lord said to Israel, "Now if you obey me fully and keep my covenant, you will be my treasured possession out of all nations. Although the whole earth is mine, you will be a kingdom of priests and a holy nation for me."

Moses received such blessings from the Lord that only Moses was allowed to go up on Mount Sinai for 40 days and be in God's presence.

Moreover, when Moses asked to see God's Glory, the Lord said to Moses, "I will do the very thing you have asked because I am very pleased with you, and I know you by name."

The above are just some of the blessings people received in the old covenant if they were obedient to God.

Jesus gave many examples of the blessings we would receive in the new covenant if we obeyed him.

Jesus said, "Whoever has my commands and obeys them, he is the one who loves me. My Father will love who loves me, and I too will love him and show myself to him."

Jesus said, "As the Father has loved me, I have loved you. Now remain in my love; you will remain in my love if you obey my commands. Just as I have obeyed my Father's commands and remain in his love."

When Jesus ascended into heaven, he sent the Holy Spirit.

It is now the Holy Spirits' job to guide and speak to us. As Jesus said, "When the Spirit of Truth comes, he will guide you into all truth. He will not speak on his own; he will speak only what he hears and tell you what is yet to come. He will bring Glory to me by taking what is mine and making it known to you. All that belongs to the

Father is mine. I said the Spirit will take what is mine and make it known to you."

Those that the Spirit of God leads are sons of God. Therefore, we must obey the Holy Spirit to receive the blessings.

I want to remind us of Psalm 91; He who dwells in the shadow of the highest will rest in the shadow of the Almighty; I will say of the Lord he is my refuge and my fortress, my God in whom I trust, surely, he will save you from the fowler's snare, and the deadly pestilence. He will cover you with his feathers, and you will find refuge under his wings. (Please read the whole psalm)

CHAPTER 12

BEING FULL OF THE HOLY SPIRIT

No one on this earth yet has received the Spirit without measure as Jesus did. (i.e., being full of the Holy Spirit). However, if we obey the Holy Spirit even in the smallest detail, we shall be given Apostolic Power.

Even when people touched the hem of Jesus' garment, they were healed; as it says, virtue flowed out of him and healed the people. When Peter walked by, even his shadow healed people.

We must strive for the same relationship with the Holy Spirit to bless others.

Jesus said, "Anyone who has faith in me will do what I have been doing. He will do even greater things than these because I go to my Father. I will do whatever you ask in my name so that the Son may bring glory to the Father. You may ask me for anything in my name, and I will do it." (I believe this is a conditional promise because in the very next line) Jesus said, "If you love me, you will obey what I command."

Moreover, again, Jesus said, "If you remain in me and my words remain in you, ask whatever you wish." However, he says if you obey my commands, you will remain in my love.

It is God's will for us to be full of the Holy Spirit and receive Apostolic Anointing, but it depends on our obedience to the leading of the Holy Spirit. When Jesus commanded, "Do not leave Jerusalem but wait for the gift my Father promised, which you have heard me speak about.

For John baptized with water, but in a few days, you will be baptized with the Holy Spirit."

How many people were not obedient and missed out on this blessing?

We should never be complacent and think we have enough of the Holy Spirit in our lives. We must continually seek the Holy Spirit and let him teach us to grow into the likeness of Jesus. Like Enoch, we can have so much of God that we do not even die but go straight to heaven. Like Elijah, we can have a relationship with God that we do not die but are taken to heaven in a fiery chariot.

Let us not short-change ourselves; we can have heaven on earth right now; it depends on our relationship and commitment to Jesus.

CHAPTER 13

Revival

IN THE BEGINNING, I shared how I went to the mainline Church in Swansea, Wales, and did not hear anything about a personal relationship with Jesus, the Holy Spirit, anything spiritual, healings, miracles, etc.

When I became a Christian, I lived in Australia and discovered things about Swansea that I had never heard while living there or mentioned in the mainline Church I went to. Just 5 miles from where I grew up in Swansea, a place called Loughery was the greatest revival the world has ever seen. It started in 1904 when a young man named Evan Roberts asked the pastor of his Church if he could hold a meeting on a Sunday Evening for mainly young people. Not many people attended that first meeting. (Guessing 9)

However, from that meeting, through the anointing of the Holy Spirit grew a revival that spread throughout Wales and most of England. (You can find the story of this revival on the website www.welshrevival.com.uk)

Evan Roberts was instructed by the Holy Spirit exactly what to say and do at these meetings. His teaching was simple: obey the Holy Spirit, repent of your sins, and accept Jesus as your Lord and Savior. The meetings would go on for hours and hours; the Holy Spirit would lead the meetings and either direct Evan Roberts to speak or someone to sing, but once the power came. (The Glory).

Then people would fall on their knees and repent out loud of their sins; people would stand up and give personal testimonies about how God had healed them or changed them. No one was in charge of these meetings, not Evan Roberts; the Holy Spirit led the meetings and instructed people to stand, speak, or sing as he willed.

Many of these meetings were not advertised, and the Holy Spirit drew people from the surrounding neighborhood, so they could not fit in the churches. In one account of a meeting, the people called on the local pastor of the Church to come to the pulpit and speak to them; he gave the wisest answer I have ever heard; he declined their offer to come to the pulpit and speak, saying he did not want to interfere with what the Holy Spirit was doing.

For those who do not know of this 1904 revival in Wales, the effect on the community was just incredible. Nearly all the pubs closed because no one was interested in drinking anymore.

They initially had a problem in the mines because the miners stopped swearing, and the pit ponies could no longer understand what they were saying. The courts had no criminals to try, and the police cells were empty.

People were aware of God in their everyday lives, which cannot be imagined today. People spent hours and hours each evening meeting, praying, and worshiping God. This revival lasted two years, but the effects are still felt a hundred years later. After two years, nearly every person in Wales was a Christian. When I lived in Swansea, it had always struck me that there were many churches in that city; now I understand why.

Another revival that I only heard about when I came to Australia was in Swansea was a man named Rees Howells, whom God told to start a Bible College. With no money, he purchased a property, and with no funds, he ran this Bible College for years. It is still there in Darwen Far, Swansea today. This bible college produced hundreds of missionaries and bible students over the years.

Reece Howells and his wife were led to central Africa, where a great revival occurred, similar to what happened in Wales in 1904. This is all told in Reece Howells's book called Intercessor.

I am telling you these things to build your Faith to understand that if you have a heart for God and his kingdom work, your city or town will have revival if you obey the Holy Spirit single-mindedly.

CHAPTER 14

God's Plan for His Church

In the Vision, I described at the beginning of the book.

Jesus explained how he wanted his Church to operate.

He wants all the ministries operating in the Church, not just the position of Priest and pastor. As Paul said in Ephesians, "It is he who gave some to be apostles, some to be prophets, some to be evangelists, some to be pastors and teachers, to prepare God's people for works of service, so that the body of Christ may be built up, until we all reach unity in the faith and the knowledge of the son of God and become mature, attaining to the whole measure of the fullness of Christ."

This scripture tells me that any church that will not allow these ministries to operate cannot grow up into the fullness of Christ. The bad news is that I have not met one Church yet that fully allows all these ministries to operate. This is because the pastor is normally afraid of these other ministries and does not allow them to operate. Also, the Priest or the pastor does not trust God and is afraid of losing control, so he does not allow the Holy Spirit to operate.

For example, I used to go to an Anglican church every Sunday, watch the Priest give a sermon, and watch the Holy Spirit open up people's hearts for Ministry as the Priest gave his Sermon. Now the people are open to God; he can operate on their hearts, but the Sermon finishes, and instead of ministering to the people, the Priest moves on to the next item of the program, and the Holy Spirit does not get to minister to the people.

I have often gone home from Church, thrown myself on my bed, and wept because the Holy Spirit was grieved that he could not minister to the people. So many people's lives could have been changed, and so many could have been helped if we just stopped our church services and let the Holy Spirit come and minister.

Pentecostal churches are not any better. There are hardly any differences between Pentecostal or mainline churches. They appear to let the Holy Spirit minister, but they do not really. They have a set format like the mainline churches, 3 or 4 worship songs, a small gap after the worship when we can have one or two prophecies, have the collection, then the main talk (Sermon), and then the notices.

I have never been to any Pentecostal church where at the beginning of the service, the speaker says we will wait on the Holy Spirit for 10 minutes today to see what he wants to do. If he instructs Anyone of you, you can run the service or do whatever the Holy Spirit instructs you.

Let us see what Paul says about how a church service should be run. What shall we say then, brothers? Everyone has a hymn, word of instruction, a revelation, a tongue, or an interpretation when you come together. All of these must be done for the strengthening of the Church. If Anyone speaks in a tongue, two or most three should speak one at a time to interpret. If there is no interpreter, the speaker should keep silent in the Church and speak to himself and God.

Two or three prophets should speak, and the others should weigh carefully what is being said. Moreover, the first speaker should stop if a revelation comes to someone sitting down. You can all prophesy so that everyone may be instructed and encouraged. The spirits of the prophets are subject to the control of the prophets.

This explanation of how churches should work clearly says that everyone in the congregation is to participate in the service. Moreover, each person will have a part to play. It does not say that the whole service is to be taken and run by the pastor or the Priest.

I know I have the instruction by the Holy Spirit to say this, and it will upset some people, but in every Church where the Priest or the pastor stands at the front of the Church and takes the whole service and controls it is in the OLD COVENANT.

I have not been in a fully surrendered church to the Holy Spirit and fully in the New Covenant, but I am sure I will one day. (I have been in one that was close)

In the old covenant, the priests are intermediaries between the people and God. Whether Pentecostal or mainline, the pastor or Priest still stands as an intermediary between the people and God.

I beg you, priests and pastors, to get out of the way now and let God back in his Church. Let Jesus be Lord of the Church; let the Holy Spirit come and take control.

Some may be thinking, why are these churches in the old covenant? As Paul says in Hebrews, now the first covenant had regulations for worship and an earthly sanctuary. (etc.), When everything had been arranged like this, the Priest regularly entered the outer room to carry on their Ministry.

If you have a priest who stands in a sanctuary and ministers, that is the immediately old covenant. That is an old covenant if your service is controlled by church traditions, set service patterns, or rules and regulations.

Even if you are Pentecostal and have set routines and rules for running the service, you are old covenant. Even if you have communion, that is an old covenant if the reason you have it is because of tradition, or we always have it at this point of the service. Anything which is not an instruction from the Holy Spirit is Old Covenant. God is looking for those true worshippers that will worship him in Spirit and Truth.

Paul explains the New Covenant God has made with us in Hebrews; this is the covenant I will make with the house of Israel after that time, declares the Lord.

I will put my laws in their minds and write them on their hearts, I will be their God, and they will be my people. No longer will a man teach his neighbor or his brother by saying know the Lord, because they will all know me, from the least of them to the greatest. For I will forgive their wickedness and will remember their sins no more.

There is no need for a Priest or pastor to run the service in the new covenant because God will make himself known to all men directly through the Holy Spirit.

Have you noticed some prophets out there why you have so much conflict with some priests and pastors? It is very simple; under the New Covenant, we are all equal or have authority as the Holy Spirit gives it. In the Old Covenant, God's Hierarchy is the Prophet and then the Priest. Moses the Prophet was in charge but not Aaron the Priest.

However, over time, the priests usurped the role of head, and when God sent any prophet to correct them, they persecuted the Prophet or had them put to death. Because nearly all the churches are in the old covenant today, it is no different; as soon as God sends a prophet to a church, some of the Priest or pastors are suddenly threatened because he meets someone who has authority from God.

I am, of course, referring to God/spiritual authority and not church/artificial authority. (There are some exceptions to this where the Priest or the pastor has a prophetic gifting and does not feel threatened when a prophet comes along)

If we want revival in the Church and the churches full of people, we must stop running our churches as old covenant churches and move fully into the new covenant.

Paul gave us the idea when he said, my message and my preaching did not come with wise and persuasive words, but with a demonstration of the Spirit's power so that your faith might not rest on men's wisdom, but on God's power.

We need the power of God back in our churches today, and the only way that will come is to repent, submit to God, obey the Holy Spirit, and hand the leadership of the church service back to the Holy Spirit.

Can you imagine what would happen if we did that? Imagine a revival like the 1904 revival in Wales. Just read in acts what God can do when people submit themselves to the Holy Spirit.

Phillip went down to a city in Samaria and proclaimed Christ there. When the crowds heard Phillip and saw the miraculous signs he did, they all paid close attention to what he said. With shrieks, evil spirits came out of many, and many paralytics and cripples were healed. So, there was great joy in that city.

Why do we not see these things happening in our churches and communities? Because the pastors and priests will not allow the Holy Spirit to come and do what needs to be done. I appeal to all my brothers in Christ, let us give God no rest until the Holy Spirit is back in control of our churches, and we can take our communities for God with the Holy Spirit's guidance and power.

I appeal to your priests and pastors to repent of blocking the Holy Spirit and let him come into your services and take control. Let the Glory come into your services, and let the Holy Spirit fill your churches. You will not need church programs to get converts; when people realize that God is actually in your Church, they will flock there to get a genuine touch from God.

In accounts of the Welsh revival, the Holy Spirit used to bring people from the surrounding area to the church meetings. When they asked people why they came, they did not know. All they knew was that something had drawn them to the church meeting that night (They did not even believe in Jesus, and they went to the church meetings)

It does not matter whether the church leaders agree to let the Holy Spirit back in the Church;

the revival has started, and a tidal wave is forming that will crash on the world shortly.

Will you be part of this tidal wave, or will you be left behind? Every move of God has a price to pay. Are you willing to pay the price? I confess that I was in rebellion with God for several years, but now I am willing to pay the price.

So, what is the price we have to pay? To turn from our sins and repent. To obey the Holy Spirit. To spend more time with God and foster a personal relationship with Jesus.

Your church leadership may embrace you or decide to persecute you. Jesus and the Holy Spirit are worth more to me than my reputation and being persecuted, and if you are obedient, God will use you.

The following are some areas that we need to deal with to come closer to God:

(I include myself in these requirements.)

1. Ingratitude (Give thanks in all things)
2. Lack of Love for God

3. Neglecting spending time with God and neglecting Prayer
4. Neglecting our bible readings
5. Lack of Love for lost Souls
6. Lack of concern for Unbelievers' needs
7. Neglecting Family Duties
8. Not being watchful over our own lives (bad habits)
9. Neglecting to be watchful over our brothers in Christ
10. Neglecting Self Denial
11. Being Worldly Minded
12. Pride
13. Envy
14. A Critical Spirit
15. Slander
16. Lack of Seriousness
17. Lying
18. Cheating
19. Hypocrisy
20. Robbing God
21. Bad Temper

22. Hindering others from being useful
23. Unforgiveness

I suggest you invite the Holy Spirit to come and show you anything on this list that you need to deal with. Only the Holy Spirit can convict you of Sin.

Remember, the motive is the most important thing about ministering in the Holy Spirit. You are just a noisy gong if you do not have to love. The purpose of the Holy Spirit is to manifest the Love of Jesus to the world.

Do we reflect the love of Jesus? No matter how powerful our gift is, it must be tested by Love for Jesus and love for souls. If we have a love of Jesus in our hearts, then we will have a love for others. Also, you cannot love others if you do not love yourself.

CHAPTER 15

Home Group Meetings

When the door closed for me to minister in churches, I held home groups for a while. These were wonderful times when many people were blessed.

The most important thing is to ask the Holy Spirit what he wants to do. If you do not get specific instruction, I suggest you not just hold a simple Bible Study. Spend some time worshipping Jesus. I used to tape music and hand out the words on a sheet so that people knew the words.

We used to ask the Holy Spirit what he wanted to teach. Sometimes he would give us specific scriptures; other times, people were led to certain topics.

Ask people to share what is on their hearts or something that might be disturbing them. Make sure you pray for each other before you finish. We gathered in a circle and put each person in the center. We used to teach the group how to pray for each other or give the word to each other. This is very easy. You listen to what the Holy Spirit puts in your mind and repeat it to the person in the middle.

If you are gathered around someone praying and get something from the Holy Spirit, do not think it is for you. The Holy Spirit will not give you something personal if you pray for someone else. Do not be afraid to speak it out, no matter how strange or outlandish. It may be some words to speak or a picture. If it is a picture, start describing it to the person, it will always mean something to them. If you are given words, even if it is just one or two, speak them out because as you are obedient and start speaking them, God will add to them.

Do not be concerned if God gives you something and someone else is speaking or ministering to the person, be patient and wait your turn, but make sure that you have your turn because what God has given you may be the most important thing to minister to that person.

Before you start your meeting, do not forget to invite the Holy Spirit to come and minister, and when you close, have a prayer thanking God for ministering and touching people's lives.

When God starts turning up at your home group meetings, it is surprising how keen people are to come.

CHAPTER 16

THE MISTAKES

THE MISTAKES ARE A very short chapter as I have not made any. (Just joking)

We are far more concerned about our mistakes than God is. If we genuinely believed we were acting on God's behalf, God would honor that and fix whatever problem we caused.

It is part of God's plan for us that we learn from making mistakes. If you look through the bible, hardly Anyone did not make a mistake. Even the Apostle Peter denied that he knew Jesus.

One reason why we fear making mistakes is that we fear Satan more than we trust God. God turns all things for good for those that love him.

Operating in the gifts of the Holy Spirit is an act of Faith. As your faith grows, so will your ability to operate the gift.

I want to speak on false prophets briefly.

There are 3 basic types of Prophecy:

1. The person hears correctly from God and delivers the message exactly as God instructed them to.
2. The person believed they were hearing from God, but it was their mind, or the Prophecy was for them, but because they did not understand it was for them, they stood up and spoke it out in the Church.
3. The person knows that the Prophecy is not from God, but to look good, they stand up in Church and speak out a

prophecy, knowing that God never instructed them to speak.

Only case 3 is a false prophet.

Case 2 is a mistake resulting from a desire to please God with maybe an immature gifting. God will still bless you because you were willing to stand up and speak on his behalf.

I would not like to be in the shoes of Case 3

I believe I have been blessed with a few mistakes in the area of the gift of Prophecy because of the following:

(a) Test the Prophecy you are given in prayer. Bind your mind in the name of Jesus, bind any power of satan in the name of Jesus, and then ask in the name of Jesus is this Prophecy from you, Holy Spirit. If I get a yes, I move on to step b

(b) Holy Spirit, is this for me or someone else. Whom do you want me to speak it to (c) When I have an answer, I move on to step c?

(c) When do you want me to speak? Is it now?

Continually ask this question right at the time you are anticipating speaking. If you never get a yes from the Holy Spirit, do not speak it out.

If you get a yes, you must speak it now (After getting permission from the pastor or Priest). If you leave speaking it out until 10 or 20 mins after the Holy Spirit instructed you—do not speak it out. When the anointing is on the words you speak, there is a power and authority absent when there is no anointing.

Be careful about overruling church authority; the Holy Spirit has never instructed me to speak a prophecy when the Priest or the pastor has said no. (But God can do whatever he pleases)

So, to some of the mistakes I have made in my Ministry, Once I worked, the Holy Spirit told me to go and speak to a Christian lady and say, "You have never fully given yourself to Jesus, just as you have never fully given yourself to your husband." I let myself talk myself out of going and speaking to this lady, and two weeks later, she left her husband, and shortly later, she left work.

I once talked to some people from work in a pub, and they were so open to the gospel message. The lady behind the bar lost a very expensive diamond ring. The Holy Spirit said to tell her it was in the bin they put the empty bottles in, and I did not like to in case I was wrong. About 10mins later, they found the ring in the bin for the empty bottles.

I tried continuing the conversation with the people from work about the gospel. Still, something had changed, they were no longer open to the gospel, and I lost the opportunity to bless them because I did not obey the Holy Spirit.

My wife had a very simple thing happen to her, she made me some lamb sandwiches, and I took them to work. She made herself some lamb sandwiches for lunch, but as she was about to eat them, the Holy Spirit said, do not eat the sandwich. My wife disobeyed the Holy Spirit and ate the sandwiches. When I got home from work, I told my wife those lamb sandwiches you made me were no good; I think the lamb was off. My wife was sick for a couple of days with food poisoning.

Once, someone in a wheelchair came to our Church, the pastor said he did not have the Faith to pray for and would I do it. I did not ask the Holy Spirit, and after a long time of prayer, the young man was not healed. I later asked the Holy Spirit, and he told me off for not asking him first and that I could have saved a lot of energy and anxiety by asking the simple question of whether he wanted me to pray for him.

As I shared in being persecuted, I disobeyed the Holy Spirit on two occasions which had catastrophic results on my Ministry. For several years all churches in Bunbury were closed to my Ministry.

Mistake (1) was the Holy Spirit instructed me not to pray for a person, and I assisted the people ministering to him, which is the same as praying for him, and disobeyed the Holy Spirit. You must be strong enough to say no to other Christians when the Holy Spirit tells you to do something contrary to their suggestion.

Mistake (2) was the following Sunday morning; the Holy Spirit spoke to me as I walked into the Church and said," whatever you do today, do not stand and speak."

I was so surprised at the personal attack launched at myself and my wife from the pulpit before the service started that I forgot the instruction of the Holy Spirit, and when I stood to speak, I was physically put outside the Church. Where the Holy Spirit promptly reminded me that he told me not to stand and speak. We must be careful to obey the Holy Spirit's every instruction, as we may not be aware of the seriousness of the situation in which that instruction is given.

I want to share that if you are given a vision, it must be exactly as the Holy Spirit showed you. I was once given a vision where three people stood at the front of the Church and gave a testimony of how God had touched them at a conference; in the Vision, I then went to the front and asked the Holy Spirit to come as a tremendous revival.

On Sunday morning, only two of the people were in Church. I prayed and prayed, but the other person did not come. The two people did go to the front and give testimony as in my Vision. I did not know what to do as it did not fit my Vision. I seemed to be getting a yes from the Holy Spirit, but I was full of doubt.

Anyway, I went to the front and asked the Holy Spirit to come. Many came to me afterward and said God touched them, but I was very disappointed, as I did not see the great revival I was expecting. I asked the Holy Spirit to explain the episode, and he led me to read a Smith Wigglesworth book.

In the book, Smith had a vision of a girl lying dead in a bed, he was there with three other people, and as he prayed for the Girl, she was brought back to life. Later that afternoon, a man came to see him and said his daughter had died. Would he come and pray for his daughter. He went upstairs, and Smith, the man, and his wife prayed for the Girl for over an hour, and nothing happened.

Smith was very puzzled and decided to give up and leave; just as he was about to leave the house, a thought came to him, and he asked the man if Anyone else lived in the house. He said yes, the Girl's grandmother was out for a walk. So, Smith waited for the grandmother to come back, and then Smith and the other 3 went into the bedroom and prayed for the Girl, and she returned to life. (The Vision he was shown was himself and 3 other people)

The Holy Spirit showed me that when God shows you a vision for something to occur, it must be exactly as the Vision, or the event will not happen.

I am sorry I cannot think of more mistakes to help you with your Ministry; I am sure I have made many more than this.

I want to signal that we are given greater revelation, understanding, and power as we progress on our spiritual journey. There may come a time when we feel superior to other Christians who are not so advanced on their spiritual journey.

This could have severe implications where we become arrogant and proud. This will affect our relationship with others where they pick up any superior attitude in their spirit and say God resists pride. Therefore, I pray that we will ensure that we remain humble and remember that everything we have is a gift from God, and we are no different or better than Anyone else. I once had a vision from the Holy Spirit, driving along on a shiny red motorbike.

I passed people in my Church walking along in the same direction. The Holy Spirit said it is unfair that they should walk while you ride. Get off the bike and walk with them. So, I got off the bike and walked along with them, pushing the bike. (of course, the bike was now heavy).

"How long do I have to walk and push this bike?" He said, "Until everyone else gets one."

So even though you know you have been given all authority and power in the name of Jesus, do not automatically assume you are to use that power but make sure you ask the Holy Spirit what he wants you to do. He might want you to get off the bike and walk.

I pray that God will bless you in your spiritual walk and that he will use you to bless others and reveal the love of Jesus to them.

CHAPTER 17

Scripture References and Notes

In the preceding chapters, I deliberately did not want to put in the relevant scripture as I wanted you to catch the teaching in your Spirit, not to analyze it with your mind.

I will go through chapter by chapter, filling in the scripture references. (Sorry if I miss any)

Introduction

If Anyone lacks wisdom, he should ask God (James 1:5-8)

Righteousness from God comes through faith in Jesus Christ (Rom 3:22)

Since there is only one God who will justify the circumcised by faith and the uncircumcised by Faith (Rom 3:30)

Chapter 1   The Vision

The marriage…(John 2:10); Apostles, Prophets, etc. …(! Cor 12:27; Eph 4:11;)

Chapter 2   Spending Time with God

Those whom the Spirit of God leads are sons of God (Rom 8:1-17)

True worshippers will worship the Father in Spirit and Truth (John 4:23-24)

I will ask the Father, and he will send you another Counselor (John 14:16)

But the Counselor the Holy Spirit whom the Father will send in my name will teach you all things (John 14:26)

Even to this day, when Moses is read, a veil covers their hearts (2Cor 3:15-18)

For God does not show favoritism (Rom2:11); Abraham meets with God (Gen18&19)

Paul meets with Jesus (Acts 9), John meets with Jesus (Rev 1)

Blessed are the pure in heart for they shall see God(Mat 5:8)

Anania and Sapphira (Acts 5); Moses rebels against God (Num 20)

The Lord met Moses and was about to kill him (Ex 4:24)

The Lord›s anger burned against Uzzah (2 Sam 6:6); Life through the Spirit (Rom 8)

Chapter 3   Being Filled with the Holy Spirit

For gifts of the Spirit and speaking in tongues, read 1 Cor 12

Being filled with the Spirit (Acts 9:17)

Receiving the Holy Spirit as a gift (Eph 1:3-16)

My Father and I will come and dwell in you (John14:20)

Receive the Holy Spirit (John 20:21-23)

Do not believe Jerusalem until (Acts 1:4-5;7-8)

And they were all filled with the Holy Spirit (Acts 4:31)

Ananias was sent to pray for Paul (Acts 9:17)

Elders in the Church in Antioch pray for Barnabus and Paul (Acts 13:1-4)

I keep asking God to give you the Spirit of revelation and wisdom (Eph 1:15-22)

Chapter 4   Being Filled with the Spirit of Elijah

I will take the Spirit that is on you and put it on them (Num 11:25)

Now, Joshua, the Son of Nun, was filled with the Spirit of wisdom because Moses had laid his hands on him (Deut 34:9)

When they arrived, they prayed for them to receive the Holy Spirit (Acts 8:15)

The Holy Spirit came on all who heard the message (Acts 10:44)

Sauls's conversion (Acts 9:1-18)

If a man›s gift is prophesying, let him use it according to his Faith (Rom 12:6)

And he will go before the Lord in the Spirit of Elijah (Luke 1:17)

Teacher, we saw a man driving out demons in your name (Mark 9:38-41)

Chapter 5   Being Baptized with Fire

He will baptize you with the Holy Spirit and with Fire (Mat 3:11)

Let me inherit a double portion of your Spirit (2 Kings 2:9)

I saw Satan fall like lightning from Heaven (Luke 10:18)

Until we put a seal on the servants of our God (Rev 7:3)

But only those people who do not have the seal of God (Rev 9:4)

The Holy Spirit Comes at Pentecost (Acts 2)

Chapter 6   The Keys to the Apostolic Anointing

I am the Lord, the God of all humanity (Jer 2:27)

And everyone who calls on the name of the Lord shall be saved (Joel 2:32)

God so loved the world (John 3:16)

Repent and be baptized in the name of Jesus Christ (Acts 2:38)

There is no other name given under heaven by which men may be saved (Acts 4:12)

I am the way, the truth, and the life; no one comes to the Father except through me (John 14:16)

Holy Father, protect them by the name-the name you gave me. (John 17:11)

Therefore go and make disciples of all nations, baptizing them in the name of the Father, and the SonSon, and the Holy Spirit (Mat 28:19)

Jesus appears to the disciples (John 20:19-23)

Jesus appears to Saul (Acts 9:1-15)

Jesus appears to John in Patmos (Rev1:9-20)

God the Father (Rev 5:1)

Look, I see heaven open and the Son of a man standing at the right hand of God (Acts 7:56)

But Stephen, full of the Holy Spirit, looked up to heaven and saw the Glory of God and Jesus standing at the right hand of God (Acts 7:55)

The Glory of the Lord (Ezekiel 1:27)

For to us, a child is born (Isaiah 9:6-7)

Unless you eat the flesh of the Son of man (John 6:53-65)

Jesus sends out the twelve (Mathew10:1)

Jesus sends out the seventy-two (Luke 10:1-23)

(2) Only the High Priest to enter the Holy of Holies (Num 18:1-7) (Luke 1:8-10)

One sacrifice for sins (Heb 10:11-18) (Heb 9:11-15)

We have the confidence to enter the Holy place by the blood of Jesus (Heb 10:19)

New priesthood-Melchizedek-Jesus now the high Priest (Heb 7:11) (Heb 8:1)

(3) New Covenant (Heb 8:1-13)

(6) One like the Son of man (Rev 1:9-19)

The rider on the white horse (Rev 19:11-21)

(8) Blasphemy against the Holy Spirit will not be forgiven (Math 12:31-32)

Ananias and Sapphira (Acts 5:1-11)

Great fear seized the Church (Acts 5:11-16)

(9) The two witnesses in Revelation (Rev 11:1-14)

Moses and Elijah with Jesus (Math 17:1-11)

The two who are anointed to serve (Zech 4:1-14)

Elijah Ministry (Malachi 4:5-6) (Luke 1:16) (Luke 3:4)

Moses Ministry (Ex 3:1-21) (Ex 4:1-29) (Deut 34:9-11) (Malachi 4:4)

(10) The Holy Spirit will teach you all things (John 14:26)

I will give you the keys to the kingdom of heaven (Math 16:19)

Chapter 7   The Gifts of the Holy Spirit

I will pour my Spirit out on all flesh (Joel 2:28-32)

Eagerly desire spiritual gifts (1Cor 14:1)

(1) Gifts of Prophecy (1Cor 14:1-39)

(2) The Holy Spirit whom the Father will send in my name will teach you all things (John 14:26)

Unless I bring you a revelation or knowledge (1Cor14:6)

If a revelation comes to someone (1Cor14:30)

(3) Your young men will see visions (Joel 2:28)

Balaams Visions (Num 24:15)

(4) Speaking in tongues (1 Cor 14:1-40)

(5) If I pray in a tongue, my Spirit prays (1 Cor 14:14-16)

(6) I saw you while you were under the fig tree (John 1:48-50)

Elisha tells the king the words you speak in your bedroom (2Kings 6:8-12)

(7) Elisha prayed oh Lord to open his eyes that he may see (2Kings 6:15-19)

(8) The Spirit lifted me and took me away (Ezekiel 3:14-15)

The Spirit of the Lord took Phillip away (Acts 8:39)

(9) The transfiguration of Jesus (Math 17:1-11)

The radiant face of Moses (Exodus 34:29-35)

(10) Anyone who has faith in me will do what I have been doing (John 14:12-13)

Chapter 8   The Works

Chapter 9   The Persecution-Being Tested

They will put you out of the synagogue (John 16:1-4)

Chapter 10   The Desert Experience

Abraham tested (Gen 22:1-19)

Do not be afraid God has come to test you (Exodus 20:20)

If you obey God, all these blessings will come to you (Deut 21:1-14)

If you disobey God, all these curses will come on you (Deut 21:15-64)

(It is interesting to note that there are more curses than blessings)

Simon, Satan has asked to sift you like wheat (Luke 22:31)

Father, if you are willing, take this cup from me (Luke 22:41)

The temptation of Jesus (Math 4:1-11)

Ananias and Sapphira (Acts 5:1-11)

Consider it joy when you face trials (James 1:2-12)

The devil will put some of you in prison to test you (Rev 2:8-10)

Chapter 11 The Blessing

If you obey God, you will be blessed (Exodus 20:20)

Blessed is the man who perseveres under trial (James 1:12)

Blessed are you when men hate you (Luke 6:22-23)

I will make those of the Synagogue of Satan (Rev 3:9)

I have prepared a table before you (Psalm 23:5)

This is my SonSon whom I love (Math 17:5)

Praise be to God who blessed me with every spiritual blessing in Christ (Eph 1:3-14)

To him who overcomes—tree of life (Rev 2:7)

He who overcomes—second death (Rev 2:11)

To him, that overcomes—manna (Rev 2:17)

To him who overcomes—Authority over the nations (Rev 2:26)

He who overcomes-dressed in white (Rev3:5)

Him that overcomes-make a pillar (Rev 3:12)

To him who overcomes-sit on my throne (Rev 3:21)

Blessings to Noah (Gen 6:9) (Gen 9:1-8)

Blessings to Abraham (Gen 13:14-17) (Gen 15:1-20)

Blessings to Moses (Exodus 24:12) (Exodus 33:17-22) (Exodus 34:8-14)

Testing at Marah (Exodus 15:25-27)

Chapter 12   Being Full of the Holy Spirit

Jesus full of the Holy Spirit (Luke 14:1)

I know that power has gone out from me (Luke 8:46)

Peters shadow healed the people (Acts 5:15)

Anyone who has faith in me (John 15:17)

If you remain in me (John 15:17)

Do not leave Jerusalem (Acts 1:4)

Enoch walked with God (Gen 5:24) (Heb 11:15)

The Kingdom of Heaven is within you (Luke 17:20-21)

Chapter 13   Revival

Chapter 14   God's Plan for His Church

Some to be apostles (1Cor12:27) (Eph 4:11)

When you come together (1Cor 14:26-39)

Now the first covenant had rules for worship (Heb 9:1-10)

Christ is the mediator of a new covenant (Heb 9:15)

This is the Covenant I will make (Heb 8:10-13)

I did not come with wise and persuasive words (1Cor2:1-5)

Phillip in Samaria (Acts 8:4-8)

Chapter 15   Home Group Meetings

Chapter 16   The Mistakes

Peter denies he knows Jesus (Luke 22:55-62)

In all things, God works for the good (Rom 8:28-39)

Perfect love drives out all fear (1 John 4:28)

ABOUT THE AUTHOR

MICHAEL SHENTON WAS BROUGHT up in Swansea, UK, in a council house estate. He originally joined the Welsh Church of England when he was 4 years old until he was approximately 14 years old.

Michael was in the Church Choir and a Server at Church Communion / Evensong for 4 years. He moved to Bunbury, WA, in 1987 and later became a member of the Anglican Church Healing Ministry Team run by Joe Hopkins. While in the ministry, Michael saw many healings and minor miracles during that time.

In 1999, God called Michael to start a Revival at St. Nicholas Church Australind, WA. He received his Prophetic Office from Paul Cain and his Apostolic Office from John Wimber.

Michael's ministry is like Paul to Timothy. He prays for people to receive the gifts of the Holy Spirit and then prays for their ministry to be in God's providence continually. He also trains and mentors the members and supports them in their ministry's needs.

Michael is not and has never been interested in the gains of his own ministry but is rather more interested in supporting and uplifting others.

Michael's ministry is very simple—he listens to the Holy Spirit and carries out whatever the Holy Spirit enlightens him to do.

Personally, Michael had met Jesus several times, not in a vision but face-to-face. Also, he had been to Heaven approximately over 30 times. This meeting with Jesus and being taken to Heaven is available to anyone, same with John and Paul, who met Jesus and were taken to

Heaven, and Michael does not see that he is any different from them.

Despite the rare opportunity of witnessing and feeling God, Michael still sees himself as no one special. He thinks anyone can do what he does if they have unwavering faith in God and a formidable relationship with Him.

Michael hopes that his experiences with God encourage you to never be afraid in seeking and creating your spiritual journey with Him.

www.ingramcontent.com/pod-product-compliance
Lightning Source LLC
Chambersburg PA
CBHW061757070526
44586CB00023B/2614